TRANSCENDING ANXIETY

A down to earth guide for transforming stress and worry through mind, body, and spirit

SABRINA JO ATTO

Dedication

In memory of two beautiful women, My mother, Lana and dear friend Kiera.

You are both loved and missed. I know you've been rooting me on from above.

Introduction

Life is full of so many beautiful moments. Ones that make us smile, laugh, and cry happy tears. Then there are those moments in life when you want to smile and laugh but you find yourself clenching your jaw or holding your breath. These are moments of anxiety where you feel hopeless, scared, tense -- and you might not even know why. This doesn't have to be your experience. There is a better way of living your life; a way of living that offers you a feeling of relaxation even when you're active, a feeling of peace in the midst of chaos. It's a way of living that empowers you to experience peace of mind.

This book includes bits and pieces of my personal journey through anxiety, and how I've been able to transform fear into love so I can live a life that offers me peace of mind and ease. The ideas, tools, and resources this book offers come from that journey and experience. They are ideas that you can work with and develop at your own pace.

The ideas I share with you throughout this book will help you shift your perspective to one that transforms anxiety rather than foster it. It includes practical tools like audio downloads for guided meditation, yoga poses, and more. Every chapter offers an idea for adjusting your perceptions and at the end of each chapter you will be able to apply the principles to your life.

My intention in writing this book is to offer a road map to anyone who is seeking a holistic or integrative approach to relieving anxiety. This book is holistic in nature, meaning it focuses on bringing harmony to mind, body, and spirit. In order to have peace of mind, there must be balance in these three areas of our life.

I can't promise that this book will help you absolve stressors from your life, or erase chaos from your days. What I can promise you is that in the midst of stress and chaos you can learn a way to live your life that will transcend all those things that harbor anxiety, allowing you to experience peace in the midst of stress and chaos. There is a peaceful way of living and you can have it. Are you ready to embrace peace? Join me as I talk about my journey and invite you to experience your own relief from anxiety.

How to Use This Book

Before you begin reading the ideas and philosophies that have helped me on my journey, I think it's important to know this:

I'm not asking you to sugar coat your life or ignore that you have real shit that's going on. I'm not asking you to smile when you're sad. No one is Mary Sunshine 24-7 and that's okay. For God's sake, I'm not suggesting you have to be a unicorn made of glitter and stardust!

I want you to know that there are tools, resources and ideas that can help you transcend mucky feelings.

Begin reading this book with an open mind. Allow what resonates with you, to resonate and what doesn't to be a suggestion. Remember you can take it or let it go.

Foster your curiosity. If something is new to you, and you feel intrigued to learn more about it, do just that. Let your instincts guide you.

Please do not feel that you have to apply everything you read in this book to your life in order to be successful at feeling better. These are tools and ideas that I've learned over many years. It is through consistent focus and work that I have been able to consistently transform anxiety.

My intention in sharing this book is to help you develop a lifestyle conducive to peace, as opposed to some new trend you try for a while then throw away.

Some chapters will have a short reflection or exercise to help you get clear about your anxiousness or mindset. Do these exercises, actually write them out with paper and pen or even use the notes section on your phone. I promise you that the benefits of writing the exercises out rather than doing them in your head is far greater and will give you lasting results.

> Visit **www.sabrinajoatto.com/book** to download resources, like a printable workbook of all the exercises in the book. You will have to enter a password to gain access to these resources. The password is **IAMPEACE** (all caps).

There is no need to try and do the exercises, tools or poses right or perfect. Putting that pressure on yourself will only cause more anxiety. There is no right or wrong way to apply these tools.

Your intention is powerful. Your will to transform your life is the catalyst for transcending anxiety. Setting the intention to do something small daily that will bring about peace is huge.

When doing the exercises, remember to take an approach that is honest and non- judgmental. When we practice these exercises, the point is to become aware of the areas of our life that can be elevated to experience life with a more potent quality of happiness and ease. There is no need to be hard on yourself or get down on yourself for the choices you are currently making or have made.

The purpose of this book is to help you transcend the areas of your life that are counterproductive and unhealthy with an approach that is kind and patient.

I'm going to strongly suggest that you take notes and highlight while you read. Jot down or mark passages or ideas that speak to you. Then every few months, or whenever it calls to you, revisit the book and reflect on your notes. In order to create a lifestyle that perpetuates peace it's important to be mindful and constant in cultivating that peace. There is a way of living that is peaceful and joyful, even in the midst of chaos. I hope you enjoy exploring this book and it is my heart's desire that you will soon be living the happy, peace filled life you deserve.

This book has been written in a very consciously conversational tone. Please imagine that you and I are just having a warm talk together. Person to person, heart to heart. . . let's begin.

My Story

I was around 14 years old when my mother was diagnosed with lupus. At the time (the late 1990's) lupus was a very new and unclear diagnosis. I remember her telling me that she was diagnosed with an autoimmune disease but that she would be fine. Prior to the diagnosis she was always tired and we couldn't understand why she always wanted to lay down and nap. The diagnosis cleared that up for us. It was also around this time that I began to experience symptoms of anxiety. I would wake up feeling nauseous, come home from school with tension headaches, and I had tight and sore muscles, among other symptoms.

I remember my family physician telling me that the symptoms I was experiencing were from anxiety and that resolving it would help heal the symptoms. However, I didn't know how to settle the anxiety, and frankly my mother, as wonderful as she was, didn't know either. The reality was that I learned a lot of my anxious tendencies from her. And her illness amplified her anxiety.

As I entered into my later teen years, I began to notice parallels between stress and physical ailment. I began to recognize that when I allowed myself to become stressed and worried that my body would display symptoms. My body reacted with pain, discomfort, and resistance. My body physically mimicked my emotions.

By the time I reached nineteen years old, I had had enough of being anxious and feeling physically ill from worry. I knew that if I didn't change my anxious ways, one day I would end up sick, -- that stress would wreak havoc on my health.

Because of the years I had watched my mother basically be a guinea pig for different meds and treatments I was anti-anything that had to do with doctors and western medicine. I went through a phase where, truthfully, I was very resentful toward modern medicine. Seeing my mother in so much pain from the side effects of her medication and doctors not knowing how to handle her illness, upset me and I found myself resenting what wasn't helping.

I've learned now that there is a place for all things and that balance between western and alternative medicines can work wonders.

Around this time a friend introduced me to the book by Louise Hay, *You Can Heal Your Life*. I was blown away after reading this book. It made sense to me instinctively that we had the ability to bring health or chaos to our bodies. I had experienced just that. I knew how stress affected me and I wanted to see how peace was going to be different.

It was then that I began reading more about holistic modalities and alternative medicines. I found myself drawn to Ayurveda, Chinese Medicine and meditation. I had become diligent in trying to unlock the mysteries of health, wellness and healing.

My mother had suggested I try yoga as she had done some yoga when she was in high school and she thought it would be great for me. My response (it was the perfect teenager response) "Hell no! I'm not doing weird bendy poses with people and 'Om'ing'. That is so weird."

Now, almost twenty years later, I'm teaching yoga. Needless to say, eventually she got her way and took me to my first yoga class.

For me yoga began as a love/hate relationship. It took me many, many years to find a practice and teachers who resonated with me. For example, vinyasa classes made me physically sick, leaving me nauseous and overheated. Being dizzy from classes almost became the norm. Then sometimes, I hated the classes that were meditative and slow, which made me breathe and ground. I found it so uncomfortable. I've since learned to appreciate being still. I've even come to crave stillness. After fifteen years of practicing on and off I found a style that I was able to practice that fostered wellness, for me. I think this is important to say because so many people have a misconception of what yoga is. Yoga is a practice that can and needs to be customized to the individual and their needs. I always suggest trying different studios, teacher and types of classes before you rule out that you don't like the practice or that it isn't for you. Even then you may find you don't like it and that's okay too.

My mother passed away when I was twenty three years old. Her passing pushed me to a deeper study of holistic health. However, it also brought up a lot of anxiety. I adopted an attitude after her passing that I wasn't going to let myself be worried or stressed. Life is short so I was going to live it to its fullest. I began only doing things that felt good to me, not caring about obligations or responsibility. I actually thought that I was living anxiety free. I was "living in the moment/in the now" like all the self-help and new age books I was reading told me I wanted to do.

What I didn't know at the time is that I wasn't living in the present. I was avoiding anxiety rather than healing it. I eventually learned that healing anxiety doesn't mean you rid challenges, obstacles or chaos from your life. Healing anxiety allows you to be in the midst of these experiences while not allowing fear and overwhelm to effect or influence you.

I was in my early twenties when I decided that the lessons I was learning, the lessons of holistic wellness, had to be shared. It wasn't for another decade that this mission became my career. I originally began working with women who were diagnosed with lupus. I went to lupus support groups meetings teaching stress reduction techniques and talking about the mind body connection. I noticed that working with this population was challenging and emotional. I decided to get more experience teaching before working with a group that brought up heavy emotions and memories for me. It took me a couple years to recognize that I connected and related best with women who wanted a holistic or even integrative approach to healing stress and worry. It was during this time of launching a wellness/spiritual coaching practice that I decided to get certified as a yoga teacher. Yoga offers so many tools for connecting mind, body and spirit that this move made sense.

That's the short version of how and why this book and my business came to be. Close to two decades of research and experience have taught me that healing anxiety may take work and persistence, but it can also be very simple. All that is needed is your willingness to make a shift from fear to love.

The Love vs Fear Perspective

One of the first lessons I learned along this journey was that our thoughts truly are powerful. Over the years, I've uncovered layers of what this truly means.

What we choose to see and believe will be our experience.

What does that mean? Tap into your green thumb goddess persona for a little clarity. Think of your thoughts as seeds. Every time you have a thought you spread those seeds to be planted. The seeds you give the greatest attention to will be the ones that grow and come into fruition.

Let's say you buy and plant basil seeds. After the seeds are planted you make sure they have sun, water and nutrients. You take the time daily to water the seeds and tend to them. Over time you begin to see budding of the plant and green starts to sprout from the soil. Eventually the plant grows bigger and stronger blooming into the best version of itself allowing you to enjoy all the best qualities of this herb.

You also bought parsley seeds but when you planted them they didn't get enough sun and you forgot to water them. You were more focused on the basil, so the parsley didn't have a chance to thrive or flower to its full potential. You might have thought about tending these seeds, but they never received tender love and care.

Your thoughts work in much the same way. The thoughts you carry are seeds. Every day you plant all these little seeds and some of those seeds take and some don't. Some seeds get eaten by birds or animals and transform, they get recycled into something new. The ones that take are the ones that were planted in good soil and well nourished.

How Do We Plant and Feed Our Thoughts?

What I've come to understand is that there are two categories that all thoughts fall under: fear and love. Fear and love are two different perspectives. How we choose to see ourselves and the world based on these perspectives will determine how we experience life. Think of perspective as the soil that the seeds will be planted in. Which of these beds you plant your seeds in will determine what will grow.

Here is a list of some of the thoughts and ideas that are associated with the perspectives fear and love.

Fear Based Thinking	Love Based Thinking
Anger	Selflessness
Greed	Surrender
Jealousy	Generosity
Insecurity	Patience
Lack	Kindness
Selfishness	Selfcare
Control	Integrity
Sabotage	Self-Respect
Lack of Self-Worth	Self-Worth
Victimization	Empowerment

The type of thought you have will determine whether or not it bears fruit and what the fruit will be. Thoughts rooted in love will always bear healthy fruit and offer salvation from anxiety and suffering.

Ultimately anxiety is fear. Learning to shift your perspective from a state of fear to one of love is the remedy for anxiousness and the discomfort that accompanies it.

Imagine your inner landscape which is the place within you that feels. It's the place that when you're happy and excited lights up and feels limitless, and that same place within you that when you are disappointed or afraid feels dark, heavy and burdensome.

Imagine in that space, at the center of your being a tree trunk that is rooted in hard rock-like soil. The tree looks dry and the branches have no leaves or flowers. The sky above the tree is gloomy and there is little or no rain to feed the tree. This is what fear looks like. Fear is lifeless it deadens our experiences. It suffocates us from life. This is how anxiety feels.

Now, turn your attention to your heart. Now imagine another tree in the inner landscape of your heart. That tree is rooted in rich soil surrounded by brilliant green grass. The trunk of the tree looks healthy and strong, the branches are full of lush green leaves and it has bright flower buds. The sky around this tree is blue, and occasionally rain is offering the tree water and the sun is offering it light. How does that place within you feel? Do you feel bright and bountiful? This is love bearing fruit.

When we choose to see things from a perspective of love, we will experience that inner tree of vibrancy and life.

I had a teacher who once said, "See is in the word seed - SEEd."

What we choose to see will be what we plant and harvest. When we choose to plant and tend love we will harvest joy, and peace, - "the sweet juicy fruit". You don't have to take my word for this. Just think of a time that you have been blissfully happy. What did it feel like physically, emotionally? Think of a time that you were relaxed and happy singing along to a song on the radio with a dorky smile on your face, not caring who saw you. Maybe it's a time you were with friends or family and laughing innocently and uncontrollably. (If you can't think of a time you were happy then I'm glad you're reading this book. We will definitely work on that!)

REAL LIFE EXAMPLES

Thought - Seed: I'm not good enough

Attention - Tending: You constantly have thoughts that your work isn't up to par, you don't look good enough, you don't deserve something great, a certain guy/girl wouldn't like you (the list could go on)

Intention: Your focus on this thought is consistent and heartfelt, you believe on some level that you lack worth.

Your Experience: You may begin to experience lack in your life, this lack can be emotional, spiritual or physical (it could be a combination of the three).

Tending this fear based thought is like watering a diseased tree. The tree has been diseased and every time you feed this perspective it spreads the disease deeper.

Thought - Seed: I am blessed (gratitude)

Attention: Keeping a gratitude journal, thanking God daily for at least one thing you are happy for in your life (this can be as simple as I have a pillow to sleep on, I have a shirt on my back)

Intention: You truly believe that you are blessed

Experience: You will experience opportunities for more

gratitude and for joy.
You will see more
things to be grateful for.
Just like tending the
basil plant allowed it to
grow big and strong, so
will gratitude yield
opportunities for joy.

What if I'm Thinking Positive and I'm Still Experiencing Anxiety and Hardship?

Thinking positive loving thoughts and living love are two different things. I can easily roll out affirmations: "I am loving, I am lovable," and not believe a single ounce of what I'm saying. Now, I'm not knocking affirmations. I do believe that they are a powerful tool if understood and properly used. What I'm saying is, thinking peace, love and happiness while gritting your teeth and cursing the driver in front of you is not transcending anxiety or fear.

Making a shift from fear to love is something that takes time. There may be instances when you're able to shift your thinking or perspective instantly. Then there will be times that you're dealing with an idea that's deep rooted. Those tangled ideas are the ones that will take some time to shift. Practicing loving kindness toward yourself is one of the greatest gifts you can exercise when healing from anxiety or stress in general.

Tools for the Tool Box

Applying What You've Just Learned

You might be wondering how to apply the information you've just read— how to shift your perception from one of fear to one that's more loving. Over the years I've learned a number of different tools and methods for making these shifts in perception.

It is important to know that not all these tools will resonate with you and that's okay. They didn't all resonate with me. How I've applied tools, and which ones I have applied has changed over time, for a number of reasons. My schedule, my interests, and my willingness have all played a role in how I chose to show up for myself.

However, there are three things that I don't suggest compromising or overlooking. These are, Awareness, Loving Kindness and Sadhana – spiritual practice. These have been my greatest gifts. I believe they can be your greatest gifts as well. If you take nothing more away from the toolbox, take these.

Awareness

Awareness is your best friend. This is one of the most important tools you will keep in your basket. Awareness is taking the time to feel and understand what is going on within and around you. When you are aware, you recognize the messages being sent to you from your body and your environment. This could be your body physically talking to you through tension headaches, aching muscles, or shortness of breath. It could be you recognizing triggers for anxiety such as, your friend, a parent, or a co-worker. Maybe an experience or subject triggers anxiety, like swimming or talking about your future.

When you catch yourself feeling anxious, worried, scared, or stressed, allow yourself to recognize the feeling. Be conscious of what is going on.

- What are you thinking?
- When did you think it?
- What's going on around you?
- Is the thought irrational?
- Is it connected to a person, place, or experience?

For some, being aware will come more naturally or easily. For others it might be challenging to connect with your body, emotions or feelings, especially if you have disconnected from yourself in order to cope with trauma. I'm not a psychologist and so I'm not going to make any medical claims or suggestions, but I would like to offer my insight. If you have experienced trauma, (for example, physical violence, sexual violence or abuse), or experienced body image issues, (eating disorder, drugs abuse, or disease), you may have, at some point, disconnected awareness from your physical body, your emotional body, or both.

If the thought of connecting to your body or emotions seems far away, illusive or overwhelming, that is perfectly okay. You can transcend that fear and eventually reconnect with these aspects of yourself if you have the will to. It is important not to put attention on when, or how long it will take, but rather keep your attention on your willingness to move forward. If this sounds overwhelming, talking to someone you trust, or a therapist could be a good place to start.

The irrational thinking I mentioned earlier is what often gets us into trouble.

Some examples of irrational thinking could include,
- Someone you're close to told you a lie and you want to write them out of your life forever because they are the worst person ever.
- You had to take a day off of work because your kid was sick and now you're going to be fired.
- You failed one paper at school and now you're going to fail the entire semester.
- A group of strangers are having a private conversation and laughing, and you think they are mocking you.
- You have a headache and you're worried it is a chronic or fatal illness.

Irrational thoughts are important to be aware of considering that these extreme thoughts trigger anxiousness.

I have put together an audio download for a guided meditation that could help you reconnect and tap into your intuitive nature - a safe place of awareness. Here is an audio download for a guided meditation at **http://www.sabrinajoatto.com/book**

If awareness is a new concept to you, start small. Even if awareness isn't new to you start small. Start with what is easiest for you.

> If bringing awareness to your body is easiest, then start with taking note of how you feel physically when tension arises or throughout the day.

> If noticing your surroundings or triggers is easiest for you start there.

> If recognizing your thoughts is the least intimidating start by noticing where your thoughts are going, and whether or not they are rational or irrational.

> Lastly, you may want to start with awareness of your emotions, of how you are feeling and why.

How you choose to approach these tools and how you use them will be unique and custom to you.

Using Awareness During an Anxiety or Stress Flare-up

1. Identify that you are experiencing anxiety or stress
2. Notice what is **physically** happening to you (e.g. tension, headache, crying, clenched jaw)
3. Notice what is **emotionally/mentally** coming up for you (resistance, anger, sadness, blame, shaming, irrational fear, irrational behavior)
4. Remind yourself that it is okay that you're having anxiousness and allow a space of non-judgment about that.
5. Don't push the experience away, rather acknowledge it, and respect that it's coming up for a reason (we will talk more about this later in the book)

Awareness will play a role in the rest of the lessons shared in this book. By simply using the steps I have outlined above, you will eventually add on techniques and ideas that will bring transcendence and healing to your anxious experiences.

You Are Your Greatest Teacher!

So, when anxiety, fear, or stress surface, bring awareness (your attention) to what is going on. You can do this mentally, verbally or even keep a journal of what you're thinking and feeling. Do what the moment calls for, do what calls to you. This moves us to the next point.

Loving Kindness

When you become aware of the anxiety or fear it's important to not judge it or yourself. This might be easier said than done. However, it is doable. This may take time and practice, but again, awareness will play an important role here as well. When and why are you being so hard on yourself? Keep in mind that there will be times that the process of transcending fear will be challenging, and it is incredibly important that you are able to be kind, supportive, and nurturing to yourself along the journey.

How to be Kind to Yourself
It might seem odd that I'm actually writing about how to show yourself kindness, but the sad truth is that we are mean and critical of ourselves daily. Below are a couple of examples of how we might be anxious, and move through it with awareness and love.

Example:
You, Being Stressed and Mean to Yourself: Augh! I have so much to do, why am I so bad at managing my time? (Maybe stress/anxiety sets in)

You, Being Aware: Wow! Okay... so, I'm stressing - I feel anxious, my chest is a little tight, my neck and shoulders are tense. I'm angry with myself, I can't seem to get my shit together.

You, Practicing Loving Kindness: It's okay that I'm stressed and anxious - I'm acknowledging it. I'm angry that my time management is not better, but this is where I'm at today. This is the person I have to work with, and this person is enough.

By acknowledging how we feel and what we are working with we begin to settle the anxiety. This acknowledgement is a form of surrender, which will be discussed in more depth later. By recognizing that who you are today is enough, it takes some pressure off the idea that you are supposed to be someone other than who you are now.

Loving kindness means offering yourself patience, self-care, compassion, and forgiveness. Practicing awareness and loving kindness toward yourself will take you far.

Imagine, awareness is like a map and kindness is the compass that leads you to peace.

What Loving Kindness is Not

Showing yourself kindness is not seeing yourself as a victim. Do not confuse self love for pity or feeling sorry for yourself. Loving kindness recognizes that you have power over the way you choose to see in a situation. It recognizes that you are responsible for your feelings and emotions and that neither others, nor, circumstance hold power over your emotions.

Sadhana

Sadhana, pronounced saa-dhah-naa, is sanskrit for daily spiritual practice. Sadhana is what you do daily to connect to spirit. This looks different for everyone. In my humble opinion, this is one of the most important tools you will ever work with. This will be your life line. I assume that if you chose to read this book you have a notion of some higher power. This higher power for some is God, Source, the Universe, Being, Spirit, Energy, Love. What you choose to call it is personal to you. I will be referencing this power as God or Source throughout the book.

Sadhana is your daily devotional -- what you do to connect with Source.

For some it is ritualistic and the same every day and for others it changes with their mood. However you choose to practice is unique to you. This includes: where you practice, what time of day, and how you practice.

Some practices that you could include in your daily sadhana are:
- Prayer
- Contemplation
- Meditation
- Journaling

See appendix for details on these suggestions.

Choosing Your Tools

I encourage you to experiment with the tools and ideas that are being offered below. You will find that some naturally call to you and others won't. Remember that this process is already challenging so there is no reason to make it harder on yourself by trying to do something you don't want to do. It won't stick.

This leads me to the idea of consistency. When you do decide on a tool that works for you be consistent with it. I'm suggesting a single tool because it is more important and potent to use one tool consistently than two or three tools inconsistently.

Once you find yourself comfortable with one tool, then add another. Take my experience as a lesson. I have a tendency to want to do EVERYTHING at once. The more I can do the better...Ummmmmmmmm! Wrong! The more you do the more diluted your efforts become. Consistency, consistency, consistency...Be consistent with whatever you choose to use.

For example, you might choose to use meditation as your first tool. You will want to set realistic intentions for yourself. If you have never meditated before then it probably isn't wise to say you are going to meditate 20 minutes twice a day. Rather, you can set the intention to meditate for 3-5 minutes daily and be consistent. When you find yourself comfortable with that, set the next intention for 5-8 minutes a day. From there you can slowly add on, gradually building to twenty minutes. This could take months or years. That's okay, there doesn't have to be some rigid set of rules you follow for relaxing. The whole point of these tools is to mellow out, not build more tension.

Tools for Peace
> Meditation
> Walking Meditation
> Yoga Nidra
> Yoga
> Working Out
> Pranayama
> Contemplation
> Journaling
> Affirmations

In the appendix, I have shared how to go about using Tools for Peace in detail including resources and an audio I have recorded for download.

Go with the tools that call out to you. If you're not quite sure which ones those are, play around and experiment with them. See which tool floats your fancy for the next few months. If you feel the need to change it up after a few months go ahead. But remember to be consistent with the tools you choose, at least giving them a few months to work.

How I First Came to Meditation

I was intrigued by the idea of meditation. To be honest one of the reasons I wanted to meditate, initially, was because I thought I would be able to party more and sleep less. This was during my twenties and a "girl just wanted to have fun". I soon realized that meditation was not meant to be a sleep substitute and not a viable reason for continuing a practice.

Eventually, I began practicing because I wanted to feel more centered and connected to spirit. I would sit alone and focus on my breath, on a vision meant to be a mantra, or a word I made my mantra. How I meditated wasn't consistent, I chose to experiment to see what worked for me.

Because I didn't have a teacher or mentor, someone who could guide me through the process, I wasn't sure what to expect and I basically left the process to itself.

There were some sessions where I felt I would drop right into the meditation, with feelings of lightness and a vibrancy that surrounded my body like I was lost in space. Then there were times my mind would wander relentlessly. I couldn't turn it off. All I wanted to do was feel that incredible feeling of "dropping into" my meditation, feeling light and relaxed.

I assumed that my wandering mind meant I wasn't meditating the "right way" and with frustration I decided I wasn't going to meditate anymore. After some time had passed I learned from multiple sources that meditation doesn't require a silent mind. It doesn't require that all thoughts cease to exist. When you think about it, that doesn't make sense...making the mind blank.

What I came to understand is that meditation is an opportunity to get still, meaning consciously making a choice to remove yourself from chaos and practice stillness. I love the word practice because it indicates that there is not performance or perfection that is taking place. It is exactly what it states, practice — applying an idea or activity repeatedly. The more you practice meditation, the more natural it becomes. Notice I use the word 'natural' and not better or easy.

Side note: There are some days that I find meditation annoying and something I don't want to do. In fact, that goes for all the tools I'm sharing with you. Just like anyone else, I have my days where I'm not in the mood to do things that are in my best interest and I would rather be a couch potato or make unhealthy choices.

What's important to remember is not making the unhealthy choices the habit and not feeling guilty if you choose to make them. I personally think guilt is more harmful than an unhealthy choice.

Meditation, or any new habit, becomes more natural the more it's practiced. It starts to become second nature. Think about something you do now that's part of your daily routine. Say, waking up in the morning and brushing your teeth. You've been brushing your teeth every morning since you can remember. This habit is so ingrained into your being that if you didn't do it something would feel off.

My take away from meditating on my own and later having teachers share their insights and knowledge is this, we each will have our own style and calling for practicing meditation. For some it may be sitting alone and focusing on the breath. For others it could be using a mantra (word, vision, symbol) that is repeated and focused on, and still for others their practice may be inclined to their religion or culture, for example the rosary (which is a twenty to twenty five minute recital of a mantra - the same two prayers repeated over and over while holding rosary bead (a sort of mala).

I share more about starting a meditation practice in the appendix.

Yoga Pose that Symbolizes the Transformation of Ego (Fear) to Love

Warrior II - Virabhdrasana II

In ancient yogic text and lore this posture, actually all the warrior postures, represent the higher self (love based self) and ego (fear based self) in battle with each other.

How to practice Virabhadrasana II Basic Alignment Cues

1. Stand with feet and arms wide (think wrists over ankles, that's how wide the feet can go).

2. On an exhale, lunge into your right knee.

3. Bring awareness to your feet. Ground through the balls of the feet, energetically taking toes forward. Keeping that action, energetically take the heels back.

4. Make sure that the knee is stacked over the ankle.

5. Keep the knee in line with the middle of the ankle and foot (think 2nd and 3rd toe).

6. Lengthen from the front body by extending navel to pubis. Breath into the back body (think kidneys/ribs).

7. Collar bone is broad, subtly bringing shoulder blades together.

8. Imagine a string at the top of your head drawing you high.

9. Allow the fingers to be soft and the gaze to be soft over the right fingers.

10. After holding this pose for anywhere from 3 breaths to 1 minute, switch sides and practice on the left side.

These are some cues that I use when guiding most students through the pose. Remember to practice in a way that feels comfortable and right for you. We all have unique shapes and conditions. If these cues or directions don't make sense in your body, remember they are simply a suggestion and one way of practicing.

SABRINA JO ATTO

♥ 2 ♥

Faith

After You Plant Your Seeds of Peace, Love, and Happiness

So, let's say you are planting awesome seeds of love. Tending the seed with faith will mean you offer it patience and space. Remember those basil seeds we planted? Imagine if you plant them and then stand over the garden where they are buried and wait for them to grow. You wouldn't do that. You know that the seedling needs time to grow. So, you tend to the plant one or two times a day. You water it and make sure it's getting enough light, you prune the garden, and maybe even feed it compost – (oooobviously it's an organic garden). You don't need to see the process of the seedling cracking open and growing roots, you just trust it will grow.

What if you felt the need to see every step of the process, the seedling crack, the sprout making its home in the dirt, then growing little roots, that eventually grow into bigger roots. Then the plant sprouting as it makes its way through the dirt, blah blah blah…. If you had to see and know every little detail that seed went through to grow into basil and then took into account all the external factors that go along with it, you would have no life. Your days would be consumed with having to know and then you would miss out on everything else that's going on around you.

Anxiety can be like this: a need to know, to understand, to control how, when, and why. What happens then when anxiety causes such a fixation whether it's about a relationship, career, or the future, is that you aren't actually living. You're hovering over that batch of soil.

Faith is the prescription for relinquishing control and trusting the process. Now, I know better than anyone that having faith or trusting the process is way easier said than done. Especially when you want to control how things turn out. So, keep this in mind... You, like the basil seed, are being nurtured and cared for by nature - a bigger Creative Source. You have the choice of where you will be buried–in fertile ground (faith) or dry undernourished soil (fear.) When you choose faith that doesn't mean that fear never pops up and you walk around all hunky dory 24/7. Fear can surface the same way weeds do in a garden.

Once you have settled into the garden of faith, you will begin to notice weeds of fear try and creep their way into your space. This is when you prune. Pruning is using the tools from chapter one and the ideas that follow this chapter (keep reading!)

How I Apply Faith to Fear

A personal example for keeping faith in the midst of uncertainty was writing this book. I've had the idea to write a book for quite a while and with my tendency to look at the end of a project and freak out because I don't know where to start it was a scary venture. Nonetheless, I made the decision to start the project, which meant looking for a writing coach. I came across a local woman, Cheri Caddick, who seemed like a good fit and made plans to meet and discuss what I was looking for. As I drove down Woodward Ave., I told myself that I was just going to talk to her, I wasn't really going to start writing the book. "I'm just meeting her and maybe I'll learn how to outline a book."

I pulled into Crispelli's Pizzeria, where we planned to meet and discuss what I was looking for. I appreciated the comfortable and casual vibe between us especially because I was so super uptight! As I sat down and we made our introductions I found myself feeling very comfortable and drawn to this woman. As we discussed the book I was interested in writing I felt my heart expand. "Oh Shit! I'm going to actually start writing this book. . . aren't I?! WTF?" That's the thought that went swirling through my mind. I found myself caught between purpose and fear.

Speaking of fear, as Cheri and I discussed how we would work together, my entire body was literally closing in. I could feel myself clenching my hands and drawing more and more inward - physically. I was about to embark on one of the most vulnerable experiences of my life and WOW I was scared.

The fear I was experiencing (and let's be honest still experience sometimes) sounded a little like this - "What do you know about transcending anxiety? Hi I'm anxiety transcend this. . . POW!" "No one wants to hear about your experiences. Don't be narcissistic!" "Your writing sucks. You have an eighth grade writing level." "People are going to know what goes on in your mind. Are you sure you want to share your inner thoughts. What if they think you're weird?"

So, how do I deal with my mean, critical, let's rub your face in the dirt ego? I allow awareness of the words I'm speaking and thoughts I'm thinking to sink in. Then, I tell my ego to F'ck off! Seriously, I'm the girl with the meme on instagram that says, "I'm spiritual and swear a shit ton," but I digress.
These fear based thoughts are like weeds in my perfectly manicured garden. Like weeds can interfere with the growth of my basil plant, so can these silly thoughts interfere with cultivating my book.

Good news, fear doesn't have to go in vain. Like weeds have some benefits (stabilizing soil and food for wildlife,) fear based thoughts are an opportunity to recognize where we need to grow, where we need to have faith. Being hung up on how the seed (thought) grows is a form of control. Controlling how the situation comes into being is not having faith. It's telling God, the universe, or nature that you know better. But guess what! You don't. Nature doesn't need us to interfere with its process for creating life. In fact, it's usually when we interfere that we stunt the process.

As for my reservations for writing a book, I took a deep look at what my fears were trying to tell me.

For example, My ego (voice of limiting beliefs): **"What do you know about transcending anxiety?
Hi, I'm anxiety, transcend this. . . POW!"**

Keeping the Faith (voice of reason): I tell myself that God's got my back. That my instincts have brought me to writing and so God will bring me through it. We aren't brought to something that we can't handle. I remind myself that the information, knowledge, insight and anything else I need during the process of writing this book will make its way to me when and how I need it.

I release a need to know the outcome of this book or the outcome of this chapter. I release the need for my writing to be perfect, or the need to satisfy the reader. I release expectations and let the process flow.

All this requires a letting go of control, which leads us to the next lesson, Surrender.

Exercise:

Where are you noticing weeds in your garden?

How can you change your inner dialogue?

NOTE: A FREE workbook containing this and all the exercises in this book is available for download from my website.

www.sabrinajoatto.com/book

Yoga Pose for Standing in Faith
Tadasana – Mountain Pose or
Samasthiti - Equal Measure

This pose represents your connectedness to the earth.

How to practice Tadasana
Basic Alignment Cues

1. Start with feet about hip/sitting bone distance apart.
2. Bring awareness to your feet. Ground through the balls of the feet, energetically taking toes forward. Keeping that action, energetically take the heels back.
3. If you have a tendency to lock out the knees maybe bend ankle, knees, hips, taking a moment to feel what the stance does in the body.
4. Lengthen the front body by extending navel to pubis. Then breathe into the back body (think back ribs/kidneys).
5. Broaden your collarbone.
6. Imagine a string at the top of your head pulling you high while the feet ground and connect with the earth.
7. Your arms will hang alongside your body with palms facing forward or palms together in front of the heart.

Side Note: Even though you're taking action and engaging the body there is still a softness to the pose. Imagine softening your skin or relaxing the face.

These are some cues that I use when guiding most students through the pose. Remember to practice in a way that feels comfortable and right for you. We all have unique shapes and conditions. If these cues or directions don't make sense in your body remember they are simply a suggestion and one way of practicing.

♥ **3** ♥

Surrender and Claim Your Happiness

Ahhhhhhhh...Surrender! This word usually makes me give off a huge sigh. I may or may not have a tendency to want to control how things turn out...

One of the greatest lessons I have put into practice is surrendering my need to have control, and frankly when it comes time to having to surrender, it isn't always a piece of cake. Sure sometimes it's easy to recognize when I'm being irrational or willful and talking myself into letting an idea go. But when fear has you by the ponytail and it feels like it's dragging and pulling you down, surrender might not be so easy. If you hang on to that fear you begin to fight and resist thinking it's the only way to get your ponytail free! Surrender is ultimately a great act of faith. Think about this:

Have you ever noticed when you allow yourself to calmly float on your back in water, your body naturally stays at the surface? But when you flail and resist the water, you sink?

Lying on your back, belly up and vulnerable giving way to the water is surrender. Kicking, screaming, and fighting the water is a kind of resistance where you eventually exhaust yourself and drown in your own fear.

Everyday life is no different. We can kick, scream and resist all that surrounds us, exhausting our resources and ignoring the natural flow (invisible force) that supports us. Or we can choose to be vulnerable, allowing the moment to be what it is and releasing pride, fear and any other mode of resistance. Notice then what happens. Eventually, the heaviness of resistance melts away and lightness comes over you. Wrinkles of tension fade from your face, your shoulders and chest fall with ease and a smile enlightens your beautiful face.

Surrender isn't losing or giving up, it is about gaining your peace of mind, and claiming your happiness. Surrender makes you a victor not a victim.

What is Resistance in Terms of Anxiety?

Resistance is a withdrawal from an experience, situation, or feeling. Rather than going with the flow or following the energy, resistance is going against the natural flow or energy. For example, say it's super windy outside and you decide to walk toward the wind. The wind is blowing towards you and you are trying to walk against it. This takes a ton of energy, leaving you struggled and fatigued. If you walked in the same direction as the wind you would find that you used much less energy. In fact, the wind would almost be pushing you forward with minimal effort on your part.

This is similar to the water analogy earlier. Life wants to naturally support us, it's our fears, false beliefs, expectations and/or need to control that would have us believe that isn't true.

Recognizing Resistance

Have you ever felt a tightness take over your whole body? It's the closing in of the eyes, tightening of the jaw, rounding of the neck and shoulders, a tightness in the chest. There's a literal drawing in of the limbs toward the center of the body. Have you ever had a tension headache? A balled up fist? A knot in your stomach? These are some physical symptoms and signs of resistance. Mental or emotional signs of resistance could show up as stubbornness, close mindedness, putting up walls/armor, or avoidance.

Applying the Principle

1. When you find yourself literally tensing up physically, take a moment to pause. Do you notice any of the mental/emotional signs like avoidance?
2. Take a deep breath using the three part breath in the appendix.
3. Ask yourself one or more of these types of questions: "What is it that I'm resisting?" "What is my body trying to tell me?" "What can I learn from this situation?" "God, what would You have me learn?" "What would You have me know?" Find a dialogue that works for you. What's important is the intention of being aware and open to seeing the situation differently. "God, how would You have me see this?"
4. If you're alone, sit in silence. Focus on your breath and just allow your self to be present.
5. Sit with whatever sensations are surfacing and allow yourself to be aware of them without judgment.
6. Listen to your inner voice, instinct, and inner knowing.

You might not feel any different after this exercise, if not, that's okay. This is a practice that is meant to be done repeatedly. The more you use awareness to ask questions and be introspective, the easier it will become to hear that inner voice or tap into your instinct.

Think of resistance as a clay wall. When clay gets wet it disintegrates. Imagine awareness as a hose and surrendering as the water. Every time you bring awareness to resistance you pull out your hose. When you practice this exercise, you begin to spray that clay wall with water—you're surrendering. Depending on how thick and high the wall is, you might have to apply this principle for quite a while before you start to see a difference. But here is what happens with each attempt at surrender: the wall becomes a little less thick, over time the clay begins to disintegrate and wash away. Eventually there is less and less wall until one day, it just completely washes away.

Practicing patience with yourself is one of the greatest gifts you can offer to you. Which takes us to the next lesson.

Yoga Pose for Surrender
Balasana – Child's Pose

Wide Leg variation with arms extended

Supported variation

Practicing Balasana
Extended Wide Leg Variation

1. You will start in table pose, coming to hands and knees.
2. Take the knees wide, you will want to feel comfortable.
3. Take the hips back toward the heels and allow the sit bones to rest on the heels.
4. Then, extend the torso forward and toward the mat.
5. Your forehead will rest on the mat or bring it to a yoga block (use a pillow/blanket if you don't have a yoga block) if it doesn't reach.
6. Arms can extend forward and rest on the mat.

Modifications: If you find that your hips don't reach your heels then you can roll up a blanket and place it behind your knees.

Supported Variation

1. You will use either a bolster or some blankets to support the body.
2. Bring bolster or stack of blankets to the pelvis.
3. Take knees wide so they are straddling the sides of the bolster or blankets.
4. Lift the sternum high toward the sky as you gently pull in your navel, keeping this subtle engagement, begin to lower the torso over the bolster/blankets.
5. Add or adjust blankets to support your body in a way that is comfortable. Maybe you add a blanket for your head.
6. Allow the arms to extend and relax.

Water does not resist.
Water flows. When you plunge
your hand into it, all you feel
is a caress. Water is not a
solid wall, it will not stop you.
But water always goes where it
wants to go, and nothing in the
end can stand against it. Water
is patient. Dripping water wears
away a stone. Remember that,
my child. Remember you are
half water. If you can't go
through an obstacle, go around
it.
Water does.

— Margaret Atwood, The Penelopiad

♥ 4 ♥

Be Where You Are

"Rivers know this: there is no hurry. We shall get there someday."
— A.A. Milne, Winnie-the-Pooh

Patience; not an easy feat in a culture that is so intent on immediate gratification. We have the internet - information at our fingertips, overnight delivery. God forbid we wait a week for our new toy. Hell, we can even order coffee or food via an app and not have to wait when we go to pick it up! All this is great! There is absolutely nothing wrong with convenience. It's important, however, to recognize that not everything in life is meant to be convenient or on OUR time.

It's easy for people, including ourselves, when giving advice to regurgitate the words, "Be patient, things will work out," "Be patient, you'll get there," "Be patient, good things take time," "be patient, blah blah blah". That's what it begins to sound like when you're anxious and fear is telling you that you need reassurance, the boyfriend/girlfriend, the degree or (fill in the blank) NOW. It's always easier to tell someone else to be patient than it is to be patient ourselves. Right?!

What I understand is that patience is an opportunity to slow down and enjoy the journey. There are two quotes that seriously put me in check when I'm wanting to rush life.

"The journey of a thousand miles begins with a single step."

— Lao -Tzu

I love food, so imagine this, you're sitting at a kitchen table, and in front of you is a huge pie - your favorite kind. You might get a plate and cut yourself a piece of that pie, then you would take a fork and put one bite in your mouth, chew that bite, swallow and then take another bite, chew, swallow, and repeat until the piece of pie on your plate was gone. I can confidently say, that most of us wouldn't dare look at the pie and expect to eat it all at once, nor would we want to.

So, why do this with our life? Why look at a situation, project, dilemma, etc and think we have to take it all in at once? This can cause some major anxiety and pressure.

Whether we look at my pie analogy or Lao-Tzu's wisdom, it's important to remember that being at peace and taking action with ease stems from being present and mindful in what we do. Being present means recognizing where you are right now, what you have to work with right now and what you can do with the time that you have right now, then taking action based on those factors.

When you find yourself wishing you had more time, gently remind yourself of what you could do with the time you have. Even if the action seems minimal and unimportant, recognize that it's not. Nothing, repeat that, NOTHING that we do is insignificant. We must take single steps to reach a destination. Do not let your critical self tell you that the little things you do each day mean nothing.

**"It is good to have an end to journey toward,
but it is the journey that matters in the end"**
— Ernest Hemingway

It is the little tiny, seemingly insignificant things we do throughout our day that create the journey of our lives. When we focus so greatly on the goal or destination we lose touch with what matters. That is, are we enjoying the journey? Earlier in the book we discussed thoughts rooted in love and thoughts rooted in fear, and how love will bear fruit and fear will leave us barren.

Imagine what kind of life you could manifest, bring into fruition, if you allowed yourself to love the journey you were on, rather than be stressed, fearful, and anxious. Take a moment and think about it. Imagine making the choice to appreciate, love, find value in the little things you do every day. How much value would this and could this add to your life?

How to Shift Anxiousness to Patience
How can we get to patience? The answer is that we practice being where we are. When I find myself anxious or wary of an outcome, I remind myself to stay present.

How to practice being where you are in the midst of anxiety:
1. Take a deep breath, maybe a few. Bring your full awareness to your inhales and exhales.
2. Give yourself a pep-talk. State what you're currently feeling and experiencing, without judgement. Be honest and real with yourself.
3. Let yourself know it's okay to feel the way you do, but that it is only temporary.
4. State the situation from an objective, non-emotional/logical perspective.

5. Let yourself know that this moment is exactly as it needs to be.

6. Put your mind in a state of Love thinking–if you can't do this that's okay, it takes time but be persistent and consistent with it.

7. Ask yourself: What can I do with what I have right now? (for example if you are working toward a goal or project: What resources do you have? What are you willing and capable of doing? What are actionable steps you can take?) e.g. I work 60 hours a week. I can make 15 minutes a day to move my body and be physically active. Another example: I work 40 hours a week, and want to write a book. I am willing to set aside 2 hours a week for writing.

8. Accept what you are able and capable of doing NOW without judgment.

9. Once you start to accept where you are and begin working from this place, rather than trying to work from a place you want to be, you will begin to notice a shift. Any feelings of stagnation will be jolted and you will begin to feel unstuck.

Side note: You're going to be doing a lot of self-talk. I promise this doesn't mean you're crazy.

How Applying this Principle Has Impacted My Life

My Love Life

Dating was never something that I found enjoyable. I always found it easier to be single and have casual relationships. (This allowed me to be in "control"). When I came to a stage in my life where I wanted more out of relationships and wanted to get married and have a family, it meant I needed to get out there and meet new people and date. If I thought about the reason I was going out and dating - to eventually get married and have a family, it freaked me out. There was a pressure that came along with that. "I have to meet the right guy. Am I going to be attracted to him? Do we have the same values? Will he get along with my friends and family?" yadda yadda...

If I stayed in this mindset of looking at the big picture, I would have freaked out and ended up avoiding or sabotaging any chance I had at being in a meaningful relationship because I was scared or overwhelmed.

When I found myself falling into these old patterns of thinking I reminded myself to be where I am.

These are Steadying Thoughts on Dating:
1. Meeting a guy is just that-meeting someone new.
2. A date with a guy is just that-a date.
3. I'm going on a date to get to know this person- no expectation or attachment to the outcome.
4. Where can I find the fun and joy in going on this date?
5. Where can I find the fun and joy in dating? What are some ways to make this fun and

exciting for me?

6. Go out and be the best version of yourself–
   don't let fear, pride, control, or other emotions
   stop you from being real, authentic and
   vulnerable.

7. What can I learn from each date and
   experience? From each interaction with
   someone new?

8. What can I offer that is of value in the dating
   world? Not "What can I gain from dating
   these men?" but, "What can I give?"

When I started to put into perspective that meeting my prince charming isn't a quest that's challenging and scary, but that it's an accumulation of everyday experiences that end up getting weaved together to one day tell a maybe beautiful, funny, interesting story the pressure lessens.

I believe one of the major keys to being present and exercising patience is to recognize that the goal isn't important, because if we were honest, the goal or objective usually changes for most of us. Even if the goal didn't change, it's significant to remember that the journey is the story we tell as to how we reached the goal. When we reflect on our life, the memories we share and recall are the everyday things we did, felt and experienced. It isn't the goal itself that holds any memory but how we reached the goal that says something. Which story is more appealing –– the one that has you smiling, comfortable with where you are, and laughing through even the most mundane moments, or the one where you furrow your brow, drudge through the day and complain to anyone who will listen while feeling heavy and unhappy? The latter is the longer darker road with all signs pointing to the first road begging you to jump trail. Follow the signs to the brighter light path. Remember, I'm not saying you won't ever have bad days or moments of grief, pain or sorrow. But you can have more happy days than not, more easy days than suffering. You can!

Take this principle and make it your own.

> **Exercise:**
> When was a time you had to take baby steps to either achieve a goal, get through a dilemma, or learn something new?
>
> Do you remember what it felt like to journey from points A-Z one step at a time?
>
> Is there an area or situation in your life right now that requires patience?
>
> How can you apply the ideas and principle shared here to your situation?
>
> What are some new ways of looking at your situation?
>
> NOTE: A FREE workbook containing this and all the exercises in this book is available for download from my website.
>
> **www.sabrinajoatto.com/book**

Yoga Pose for Practicing Patience
Tree Pose – Vrksasana

Yogic mythology talks about Sita, a yogic diety, sitting under the ashoka trees after being kidnapped by Ravana. She waited patiently for her love, Rama, to find and rescue her. This quote by Zo Newell says it best, "Trees are patient creatures. They live a long, quiet time and know how to stand firm through all the changes of the day and night, climate and season."

Trees know how to just be.

Here are two variations of Vrksasana

How to practice Vrksasana
Basic Alignment Cues

1. Come to Tadasana (Mountain Pose).
2. Take your gaze to a spot on the ground in front of you that isn't moving. Connect with that spot.
3. Bring attention to your breath and draw your energy from the outer edges in toward the center of the body.
4. Imagine squeezing a block or ball between your thighs. This is the action of drawing energy toward the midline.
5. Bring your right foot to your right ankle or shin keeping below the knee, or help it to your thigh keeping it above the knee (avoid direct contact with knee you don't want to put pressure on the joint).
6. Once the foot is positioned, lengthen front body by extending navel to pubis, then breathe into the back body.
7. Broaden your collar bone.
8. Imagine a string at the top of your head pulling you toward the sky.
9. Allow the hands to be in front of the heart, on your hips, over head, or maybe the hands are at the wall for support.
10. Practice for 3 breaths or hold for as long as you can, trying to maybe hold for a full minute.

Practicing this pose, for me, fosters patience. It's a pose that changes all the time. Some days I can hold this posture with ease and steadiness while other days I'm lucky to get my toes off the ground without wobbling. It fosters patience for me because it teaches me to be where I'm at today, not where I was yesterday not where I want to be today or tomorrow but accepting where I am in this moment and what it means.

With patience comes kindness...

♥ 5 ♥

Be Your Own Best Friend

Doing personal growth and spiritual growth work can be very taxing. Taking a look at your deepest darkest fears isn't for the faint of heart. It's easy to get caught up in doing the work of applying the principles in this book, being aware and confronting your fears, and thinking that you should be over your anxiety because it's been 1 month, 1 year, or 10 years. Growth doesn't work that way. In fact, we never stop growing. There will always be new lessons to learn, and new ways to learn them. As for anxiety, the things that would normally trigger your anxiety will begin to fade. The way you react to stressors will be different. Actions and reactions will begin to change, and because of this change you will experience life differently. This doesn't mean that you will never have moments of anxiety. What it does mean is that you will react differently to the anxiety. It will no longer control you or manipulate you. Rather, you will be able to look at it objectively and come through stronger for it.

What is so important to remember along this journey is to be kind to yourself. Offer yourself patience and time to heal the anxiety. If you're anything like me, it's crazy easy to be critical and hard on myself, expecting changes and results that aren't realistic.

Why Kindness Trumps Criticism

Recall a time you were yelled at or criticized. What was your initial reaction? Did your body tighten up and close off? Did you get defensive? Did you feel angry? Judged? Attacked? When this happens we build up walls of defense. That's the natural response when you feel you're being attacked. Those walls are walls of fear. Fear, because you felt attacked and needed to defend and protect yourself.

What if you flipped the script? What if instead of being critical and hard on yourself, you treated yourself with compassion and love. You would be kind to yourself. Recall a time when you felt good and genuinely happy. Think of a time that you were singing along to your favorite song, belting out the words not concerned with anyone hearing you or judging you. That feeling of openness where the heart and body feel light is the result of being kind to yourself. Being kind to yourself is a habit you want to get into.
And remember, if we are constantly pointing out our flaws, shortcomings and missteps, we are missing moments to celebrate our triumphs and growths.

Practicing Kindness Especially When it Comes to Personal Growth

Our intention with healing anxiety is to break down walls of false protection and erase limiting beliefs. If we aren't being kind to ourselves then we are reinforcing that which we are looking to undo. Personal growth work is heavy. We are asking ourselves to look deep into places that are dark. The dark is a scary place for most people. In order to build courage and strength for that journey of self exploration we must tell ourselves how wonderful we are.

Now, I know some of you might be thinking, "I'm not wonderful,

I'm not strong, and I can't do it." And I say STOP RIGHT THERE! If you picked up this book and you're reading it you have courage and you are strong. It takes a strong and brave individual to want to do good for themselves, to choose to confront something that challenges them. That is exactly what you are doing right now by reading this book. You are confronting a challenge and making a choice to work through it.

Pretend It Isn't About You

Think of someone who is physically ill. What words of encouragement would you give them?

Think of someone who is going through a transition in life that is challenging and you want to be supportive. How would you talk to them?

Think of a child who is learning something new. How would you talk to and encourage them?

The way we choose to speak to ourselves is so important along this journey. Choosing words of compassion, patience, and encouragement are going to make this journey of healing go by so much easier and faster.

Shifting from Criticism and Fear to Kindness

1. Become aware of when you are being hard on, or criticizing yourself.
2. Consciously ask, "What is another way of seeing this situation or myself?"
3. Rephrase the dialogue (i.e. "I'm so stupid." Shifts to, "I could have done 'A' instead of 'B'. Can I change or fix this? If not, what can I take away or learn from this situation?"

Being kind to yourself along this journey of exploration, discovery and healing means you recognize that every situation is an opportunity for growth and learning. It means that you allow yourself to be a student and don't judge yourself for being a student.

Imagine entering a dark room and you can't see anything. So you stand in the room for a few minutes and your eyes begin to adjust. You see shapes and shadows but can't fully make them out. Maybe you panic because you think there is a threat in this dark room and you don't fully know what that threat is capable of. The longer you stand in this room the more your eyes begin to adjust. Eventually, you make your way to a wall and begin to feel for a light switch. As you feel your way through the room you are able to make out some of the items and you begin to feel familiar and even safer in this space. But you're still a little frightened because you can't see everything and you still feel threatened. Eventually, you do find a light switch and when you flip it on you notice that the shadow you thought was a threat was only a stuffed animal and a lamp behind it.

Working through anxiety is very much like entering a dark room. The anxious feelings you are experiencing are dark aspects of yourself. When you have the courage to walk into this dark space, confronting the fear and give yourself time to adjust your "vision" you will start to see things for what they truly are. By bringing love, kindness, and compassion to this dark space you are bringing light. That light will eventually illuminate what was once dark, scary and threatening. When you allow the light to FULLY shine through that dark space you will always find that there is no threat. And what you once feared will no longer hold you.

How You Can Tell You're Being Kind to Yourself
You know you're practicing kindness and showing yourself love

and compassion when you feel a sense of relief. When the physical tension in the body begins to lighten and you soften any holding or clenching. When you're showing yourself love you will feel like what you are doing now, today, in this moment, is good enough.

Applying this Concept: Ways of Practicing Kindness

1. **Take a Compliment:** One way of embracing love and kindness is to accept it from others. Notice how often you actually take a compliment and embrace it and notice how often you actually reject compliments when they are given. No matter how insecure you might feel remember to always accept a compliment.

Example 1

Friend:	"Your dinner was so delicious. I loved the pasta you made!"
Critical You:	"Augh, I didn't have all the ingredients. It's usually way better than that."
Kindness Shift:	"Thank you, I'm so glad you liked it. I usually add cream to the sauce but didn't have any. So glad to know the recipe can be delicious both ways."

Example 2

Co-Worker:	"You look so cute today. I love that dress."
Critical You:	"Really? I've gained weight and this is my frump dress!"

Kindness Shift: "Thank you. That
                    compliment was just what I
                    needed to hear!"

The first responses are ones that reject a compliment, in turn rejecting love for you.

Exercise:
Goal: Embrace the Love!

When was a time you were given a compliment and turned it down? How could you have rephrased your reaction to be more kind?

NOTE: A FREE workbook containing this and all the exercises in this book is available for download from my website.

www.sabrinajoatto.com/book

2. Accept Generosity: Allow others to do nice things for you, accept help when others offer it.

Example
Spouse: "You've been really busy
                  this week, what can I do to
                  make things easier for
                  you?" (okay, if you're
                  dating or married to
                  someone who actually asks
                  this, hold on to them...just
                  saying)

"In Control" You: "I've got everything under control. I don't need help!"

Kindness Shift: "Thanks, I could use some help with putting the laundry away." (I feel like half the women reading this are mentally saying I hate how he puts the laundry away. It doesn't have to be the laundry, you get my point.)

Give yourself permission to not be a super hero! You don't always have to have your shit together.

Exercise:
When was a time you tried to be a super hero? How could you have slowed down and asked for or accepted help?

NOTE: A FREE workbook containing this and all the exercises in this book is available for download from my website.

www.sabrinajoatto.com/book

3. Give Yourself Permission to be mediocre or even bad at something.

Example
Critical You: "I suck at giving presentations."

Mentor:	"Everything takes practice, the more you give presentations the smoother they will become."
Critical You:	"I'll never be good at them; I hate getting in front of people and presenting."
Kindness Shift:	"I'm afraid of giving presentations. What advice do you have for me to strengthen this skill?"

This shift gives you permission to make mistakes and learn, it takes the judgment of failure off the table.

Exercise:
When was a time you put pressure on yourself to be better than you were? How could you have accepted where you were and still nurtured the desire to grow?

NOTE: A FREE workbook containing this and all the exercises in this book is available for download from my website.

www.sabrinajoatto.com/book

A Yoga Mudra for Cultivating Kindness
Padma Mudra – Lotus Seal

This mudra, hand gesture, symbolizes the emergence of light from dark, an opening and purity of the heart. The lotus flower sits in its full beauty floating at the surface of water. What we usually don't see is that it's rooted deep into the mud.

Like the lotus flower, we too have the ability to grow from darkness and emerge into the light.

How to Practice Lotus Mudra
    1. Begin by bringing the base of the palms together.
    2. Next, bring thumbs and pinkies to touch.
    3. Finally, allow other fingers to fan open.

Using This Mudra with a Visualization Meditation
    1. Bring your hands to Lotus Mudra and hold in front of your heart.
    2. Allow the eyes to close or soften your gaze.

3. Imagine now any darkness, limiting beliefs, or words of criticism rising out of the heart space into the lotus mudra.
4. As this darkness travels up see and feel it leaving through your hands as light.
5. Imagine that light showering over you, washing you with love.

Hold this visualization for as long as you feel you want or need to.

♥ 6 ♥

The Power of Intention (Sankalpa)

Sankalpa is a Sanskrit term that means resolve or resolution. It can also be thought of as intention. There are a couple different ways I've found using a sankalpa to be useful. The first way is to set an intention or resolution for my day. There are some mornings I wake up on the wrong side of the bed. If I'm lucky I catch this low mood right away and work on shifting it before I leave my house. If I'm feeling stubborn and a glutton for misery, then it might take me snapping at a few people or cursing traffic on my way to work before I get it together. When I finally do get it together it's because I've resolved or intended to see things differently. I might say aloud or to myself, "How can I see this day differently?" then I'll set my sankalpa: "I intend to look at this day with gratitude." or maybe "I intend to be kind to each person I encounter today."

These simple resolutions help to shift me from a mood that is low, ornery, or stressed to a more vibrant, pleasant, happy state. These two examples: "I intend to look at this day with gratitude," automatically takes you out of a lack mentality and into an appreciative mentality. How can you be sad, stressed or angry when you're grateful? Try it, I bet you can't stay in a low mood!!! And the second example, "I intend to be kind to each person I encounter today," is almost immediate after the first few people you smile at and genuinely show kindness to, you won't be able to stay in a funk! Your mood lifts and you actually start to show yourself kindness.

Another way I use sankalpa is to set a resolution or intention for a project, task, relationship, etc that is causing my anxiousness. For example, just this week I was asked to appear on television for a yoga program that would air on cable community television. I was hesitant to say yes because I didn't know if I could pull off being on television, but I often challenge myself to confront my fears. This was one of those times. I told myself that if the opportunity presented itself it's because I was ready for it. As the days got closer to filming the segment I found myself anxious. As I planned for the event I decided to set a sankalpa. I stated that "I am prepared to the best of my ability and giving this 100 percent. This is an opportunity to grow and learn. I'm kind to myself as opposed to overly critical or judgmental." I did have some lingering nervousness which is totally normal. It's okay to feel nervous. In fact, a little bit of anxiousness can be healthy it keeps us on our toes. What we are aiming to relieve is anxiety that stunts or paralyzes us, or causes somatic symptoms in the body.

Setting a Sankalpa
Here are some general rules or guidelines for setting a sankalpa.

• State in the Present Tense

Always make your statement as if it has already happened or happening. By setting in the present you are confirming that it is already taking place or in action.

Incorrect: I will be kind to every person I encounter today.
Saying "I will" implies the future. When will you start? It's not concrete.

Correct: I intend to be kind to every person I encounter today.

"I intend" is intention in action. It's happening right now. It's a solid statement of taking action and follow through.

• Keep It Positive

What we put our attention on grows. By focusing on the positive we move toward the positive.

Incorrect: I am not critical of myself.

How does this sound to you? Say it out loud, then listen. It feels heavy right? By stating you are not critical puts attention on criticism. You've said critical and now critical is on the mind.

Correct: I am kind to myself.

Just making this statement feels so much lighter than the former statement. "I am kind." You are telling the mind that you are kind this is what it will recall every time you make the statement.

• Make the Statement From Your Heart

When we set an intention, it's power comes from speaking it with truth and "heart". When I am looking to connect to my heart and truly set a sankalpa or even pray I do this:

1. Completely relax-starting with softening tension from the scalp all the way down the body.
2. Bring full awareness to the breath.
3. Bring awareness to each heartbeat.
4. Bring the hands to the heart and feel each

heartbeat.

5. State the sankalpa and hold it in this heart space.
6. Sit with awareness here for a moment.
7. Then leave the statement in your heart, and go about your business!

• Repeat the Statement Regularly

Remind yourself of this resolution throughout the day, the hour, any time you feel yourself slipping into a state of stress, anxiety, or low energy. You can close your eyes and bring your attention to your heart and recall the message you left in this space. You may notice a shift once you recall the message you left with your heart.

Here are some example of sankalpas that you could use to lift your mood, reduce stress and anxiousness, and calm the mind.

Note: When making these statements you want to believe them on some level. I've been told fake it til you make it. That approach hasn't worked well for me. If you're able to fake something til you make it...GREAT, by all means go for it. But if you're like me and need to believe what you're saying then choose a sankalpa that makes sense to you. You always want the tools and techniques you're going to employ to resonate with you, this will ensure their effectiveness.

Examples of Sankalpas

"I intend to be kind to every person I encounter today."
"I intend to practice gratitude toward all things I do and say."

"I am kind and loving to myself. I see my abundant worth and value."

"I am calm and centered, I take reasonable steps and actions toward my goals."

"I confront my fears and shine light on it's darkness." or "I confront my fears and illuminate that which is dark."

"I surrender my fear, worry, anxiety to God and allow him to transform it through grace."

"I love the work I do and move forward with ease as I accomplish today's tasks."

Crafting Your Own Sankalpa

Play around with setting some sankalpas of your own!

Exercise:
Ideas for keeping it in the present tense:

I am...

I intend...

I confront...

I take action...

I move forward...

I love...

I surrender...

I resolve to...

Practice crafting your sankalpas

NOTE: A FREE workbook containing this and all the exercises in this book is available for download from my website.

www.sabrinajoatto.com/book

A Yoga Mudra for Setting a Sankalpa (Intention) Anjali Mudra

You may hear this mudra referred to as namaste hands or prayer hands. Anjali is Sanskrit for divine offering. You can also think of it as a gesture of reverence.

How to Use Anjali Mudra when Setting a Sankalpa

1. Come to a comfortable seat.
2. Bring the palms of your hands together allowing them to rest in front of the heart.
3. Take a few deep breaths as you begin to get grounded and centered.
4. Bring attention to your heart, maybe even connecting the thumbs to your sternum.
5. Take a moment to feel your sankalpa (intention).
6. When you've connected to the feeling allow your heart to pray or sing the intention.
7. You can state the intention once or three times if you like.

♥ **7** ♥

Being of Service

"We become happier, much happier, when we realize that life is an opportunity rather than an obligation."
—Author Unknown

When we look at our life as a responsibility, be it our job, family, or home, it can start to feel burdensome. There is a plaque I bought years ago from Homegoods because I loved the message painted on it. It reads "We become happier, much happier, when we realize that life is an opportunity rather than an obligation." Whenever I catch myself feeling heavy about work, obligations or other worldly responsibilities I remind myself of this message. There are different ways I choose to interpret opportunity. One of those ways is to recognize that I have an opportunity to be of service to God. This means that my actions aren't for me, my family, or friends, they are to serve something greater.

Just this week I was teaching one of my weekly yoga classes. I normally set an intention at the beginning of class to align myself with Source. This particular class I asked the students to set their intention but I didn't set mine. For whatever reason I forgot to set my intention. As I began to teach I found that I wasn't really into teaching the class. I was teaching out of obligation because I felt like this was my Thursday morning class and I had to be there. I almost immediately picked up on my energy. I knew I wasn't connected. I knew at that moment, that I had lost sight of why I was teaching yoga. I silently reminded myself that I was there to be of service to these students. I wasn't there to simply fill an hour and get a paycheck. I was there to offer them an opportunity to escape stress, chaos, tension. Once I made that shift mentally, then from my heart, the class took on a whole new meaning and experience for me. The students may or may not have picked up on my energy. But the point is that my feeling of obligation was shifted to one of service and it altered how I experienced that class.

This can be applied to all areas of our lives.

What a Service Mindset Feels Like
Can you think of a time when you were consumed with how a situation was going to affect you? You might have been consumed with how you would feel, what you would gain, how you would benefit, etc. How did that pressure make you feel? I know for me it can be an anxious feeling, not knowing what to expect. Physically I might feel tight/tense, small, restricted, and nervous. Can you think of a time when you were selfless, you offered yourself to the service of someone else without any expectations or strings attached? How did you feel? Usually when we don't have expectations, and we take action for the sake of love we feel light, unburdened, and expansive.

Why Being of Service Eases Anxiety
Service is another way of moving away from the self and recognizing that you are part of a whole. Think of humankind as a living, breathing body and each cell represents all other beings. In a body, if each cell only sought to function for itself the body couldn't function properly. There would be disease and chaos within the body. On the flip side, since every cell functions to serve

the greater whole, it's functions harmonize the body. If you recognize that your purpose is not to serve yourself but to serve the greater whole you begin to experience that lightness, expansiveness and ease in your actions. Because you are no longer cultivating chaos, you are cultivating harmony.

Being of service doesn't mean you put yourself last or neglect your needs and desires. It means more that you start to align your desires with something Divine.

Apply This Idea: Being of Service

Exercise:
Take a moment to think of areas in your life that cause you stress and anxiety. Write down those areas.

Examples:
1. I work at a law firm, things are chaotic and stressful. My workload is overwhelming.
2. I'm home all day with my kids and feel neglected, tired, and burned out.

How can you see these areas or responsibilities as an opportunity to serve God?

Examples:
1. I work at a law firm that specializes in divorce. I have an opportunity to offer love and kindness to those who are going through a difficult transition.

2. My children aren't my obligation, they are a
   gift. I have an opportunity to offer them the
   best of who I am so they can be the best of
   who they are meant to be.

Perceiving any area of our life as an obligation, responsibility
or duty can cause undue stress or flare up anxious feelings,
especially if it isn't something you want to be doing. Learning
to shift our perception to one of service lightens our load. It
takes the responsibility factor out and sets the precedence for
something great. Your time is now being spent doing good,
being helpful, and serving a greater purpose.

NOTE: A FREE workbook containing this and all the
exercises in this book is available for download from my
website.

www.sabrinajoatto.com/book

♥ 8 ♥

We, Not Me

Have you ever noticed that when you're anxious and fearful of an outcome it's because you're focusing on yourself. Notice if your dialogue sounds like this, "How am I going to get through it?", "How am I going to accomplish it?", "How am I going to perform?" Next time you're anxious, take note of your inner dialogue. If it's "me" and "I" oriented know there is another way to look at the situation. This is by recognizing that you don't have to do things alone. There is a Source or Power that has your back. When we choose to align ourselves with this Source and acknowledge that it's through this Source that all things can be accomplished we lighten the load we've put on our shoulders.

If you knew that you had a Source that was all powerful and could accommodate for all things would you not feel less stressed or burdened when carrying out life's experiences big or small?

This is a big topic, aligning with God and working with Divinity as a team. It's a topic that deserves its own book. So without going too deep into this area, I would like to offer you this tool or idea. You never have to be alone, and when you feel alone, know that all you have to do is ask for help. One way of shifting from a self-centered dialogue to an inclusive dialogue is to become aware of every time you use the word "I" and replace it with "We".

Then, imagine this Source (whether it's a big ball of light, an angel, a person, or whatever resonates for you) is literally by your side, guiding and supporting each step or movement you take, each word that you speak. Believe that this Source has literally and figuratively got your back.

If you haven't picked up on it already, you will...I'm a quote person and there is this quote that I absolutely love.

"Those mountains you are carrying, you were only supposed to climb."
—Najwa Zebian

When I first read this quote it landed hard, in a good way. I thought, "Wow! How true, we take what is meant to be an adventure and make it a burden!" One of the ways I believe we do this in our lives is by thinking or believing that we have to do things on our own and that we have to rely on our own abilities, studies, and experiences to get through.

What I've come to understand is that when we choose to focus on our own abilities, talents, merits, etc. we are limiting ourselves. These limitations can cause anxiousness. After yoga teacher training, I had to teach a feedback class where my teacher and fellow students would critique how I taught. I was so nervous leading up to this testing. I didn't know what to expect. My default was to compare myself to teachers with way more experience and schooling than I had. So, instead of allowing old patterns and beliefs to turn the volume high on my anxiety, I decided to take deep breaths, play some calming music and gently remind myself that I didn't have to do this alone. I chose to be where I was at. **Then I used the mantra "We can do it!"**

This is a mantra I use daily. "We" recognizes that God or Source (whatever you reference as Higher Power) is working with me, side by side.

Whenever I catch myself using a phrase like, "I have to..." "I need to..." "I'm responsible for..." I shift my language and replace that I with We, "We have to..." "We need to..." "We are responsible for..." This simple shift takes the mountains off your shoulders so you can actually climb them. Rather than being burdened you're giving yourself an opportunity to have an experience.

Everything is Sacred or Nothing is Sacred

I had a teacher whose lifestyle truly impressed me. Over a nine month journey with this particular teacher I noticed something significant, something I wanted to adopt for my own life. She infused the Divine into everything she did. Why did she do this? She saw everything as sacred. What she said, what she wore, how she ate, how she held herself, how she arranged the room before a meeting, class, or retreat all held an importance, a special meaning. Because she saw life as sacred, she was able to bring the Divine into everything she did.

Albert Einstein said, "There are only two ways to live your life. One is as though nothing is a miracle. The other is as though everything is a miracle." I think this statement hits the nail on the head. I also believe that it can be translated to *There are only two ways to see the world. One is as though nothing is sacred. The other is as though everything is sacred.*

It's easy to take our daily life for granted. Most of us do. We get caught up with friends, gossip, what's hot and trending, pop culture, politics, and the list goes on. One way to start infusing Divinity into everything you do is to find the miracle in what you're doing.

For example, let's use the teacher I mentioned earlier. When she is setting up for a meeting she is conscious of setting up the chairs, blankets, food, and supplies with purpose and meaning. Rather than just throwing the room together before people made their way to the meeting, she and her assistants made a point to put their hearts into what they were doing. They didn't just throw chairs together in a circle, they placed the chairs in a circle with love and excitement.

Almost every year, I host Thanksgiving for my immediate and extended family. I LOVE to cook so this is a lot of fun for me. I get to plan a new menu each year, try new recipes, and put a fun spin on a traditional Thanksgiving dinner. When I'm planning this holiday I'm constantly reminding myself that how I prepare the meal is going to be how my guests experience the meal. One way I align myself with God in preparation for hosting this day is to get excited and find the joy in planning. Next, I call my cousin Brittany who is one of the few people I actually allow into the kitchen with me. I like me space when cooking! Because Brit and I work so well together in the kitchen it makes it so much fun to bounce ideas and recipes off one another. (Keep an eye open for our cook book one day!) Usually she'll come over the day before Thanksgiving and we put on Christmas music maybe have a glass of wine, hot tea, coffee, or all three depending on our mood and we prepare and prep the meal.

Being in line with high vibes and happy energy is a way of aligning with the Divine. Bringing the sacred into your daily life doesn't have to be a ceremony or something super spiritual. Sometimes it will be, but other times it's just going to be infusing what you do with love and tenderness.

Bringing Awareness to this Idea
What reminds me of this principle is my dialogue, am I using "I"

a lot? Am I relying on my own merits? When I catch myself in this pattern, I make a conscious shift. If that kind of awareness isn't helpful for you, you could create a practice that might better serve you.

For example:
- Place post-it notes for yourself around the house, car, work that have little messages to remind you to align with God or Source.
- Start and end your day with a prayer, poem, or intention that aligns you with Source.

Practicing This Principle

Exercise:

Write down three things you have to do or have going on that are bringing up stress/anxiety.

Example 1:

I have to finish cooking this meal before company arrives.

Example 2:

My career depends on this meeting going well, I can't F@*# Up!

Reconstruct the phrase so that it includes God as part of the statement.

Example 1:

We will finish this meal in the perfect time.

Example 2:

I am connected to God/Source/Divinity, I approach this meeting aligned with Greatness so all things go well and the best outcome arrives.

NOTE: A FREE workbook containing this and all the exercises in this book is available for download from my website.

www.sabrinajoatto.com/book

♥ 9 ♥

Ayurveda: Sister Science to Yoga

I sat down with my friend Natalie who is an ayurvedic practitioner with the intention of getting super technical about what ayurveda is and how it can help you alleviate anxiety. As we sat down to talk about the book and this ancient practice, she began by asking me a series of questions. I wasn't expecting this. I was supposed to ask her questions. Hmmmmm.

As we began talking and she probed about my experience with ayurveda it dawned on me. Ayurveda, technical as it can be, is experiential. I'm pretty sure she was purposely pushing me to wake up to this realization. So rather than breaking down the biomechanics of this unique science, I would like to share my journey and discovery of the practice that is over 5,000 years old.

Wait! Ayur...What?

Ayurveda pronounced ah-yer-vey-duh, is the sister science to yoga and is a holistic medical practice that dates back over 5,000 years. The practice recognizes that all aspects of life and all humans are unique and individual, but also connected. It's a science that sees mind, body and spirit being interconnected.

My Introduction to The Yoga Science & It's Influence
I remember first being introduced to ayurveda in the early 2000s.

I read articles on Care2.com from Deepak Chopra and he referenced ayurveda. In response to one of the articles, I took an online quiz that determined my unique constitution. In ayurveda, there is the understanding that we are made of the same elements as nature:

- Ether (Space)
- Air
- Fire
- Water
- Earth

Theory says that each of these elements carries with them unique qualities that can bring harmony or disharmony depending on how they are brought together.

The Dosha quiz, determined that my constitution, although made up of all the five elements was predominantly fire with a little water. This dosha is considered Pitta. I began researching what it meant to be pitta dosha. My research led me to foods that pacify and aggravate pitta. And so, I experimented with some different foods and decided I wasn't interested in this science. With the very little knowledge I had regarding ayurveda it seemed complicated, and truthfully, I hated the idea of not eating certain foods I loved.

Years later I met my friend Natalie and I was desperate to find a way to clear up blemished skin. I had tried everything under the sun to clear up break outs and no matter what dermatologist I visited or esthetician I saw, they all said the same thing. "Your skin care routine is perfect, your diet is clean, and you work out, I don't get why you keep having break outs." Natalie and I were on a retreat for a women's group we were a part of and I remember asking her if ayurveda could help with skin conditions. Her answer was YES!

When we began working together she helped me to understand that even though ayurveda has lifestyle "rules", for diet and exercise among others, it is really suggestions for cultivating balance. When I first learned of ayurveda I thought the dietary "restrictions" that I had read were black and white, that I couldn't eat foods on the avoid list, and had to over eat foods on the "good for pitta" list. I've discovered through working with Natalie, both privately and during her biannual cleanse, that ayurveda doesn't support extremes. Instead, it's a practice that supports finding what works for you and finding harmony.

It was the discovery that ayurveda wasn't a strict rigid set of rules that opened me to learning more and a desire to incorporate it into my life. I felt relieved that I didn't fit into a neat little box and that medicine and wellness didn't fit into a neat little box. The idea that we are each unique and that every day is unique was liberating for me.

My Relationship with Food & Ayurveda

I love, love, love food. I enjoy cooking and eating. Food has played an important role in my life. It has been a way that my family has come together. It was Sunday dinner at my grandma's as a kid, my mom making my favorite meal, holidays, or a casual phone call from an aunt that says, "I made dinner. Come over." Food is also one of the ways that I find myself socializing with friends as we gather in someone's kitchen, crack open some wine and snack on cheese – does it really get any better? These are nourishing memories surrounding food. The less nourishing ways I've used food is to soothe discomfort or eat out of boredom.

Ayurveda has brought me awareness of when I'm using food in a way that can and will cultivate wellness, and when I'm using food in a way that is unhealthy.

During a cleanse, Natalie shared a bit of wisdom from one of her teachers. I'm paraphrasing, "Americans have so much knowledge about what's in food: nutrients, vitamins, calories but what they don't understand is what it means to be empty." WOW!

This statement really impacted me because it was my reality. The thought of being empty was a bit unnerving, I had become accustomed to eating when I wanted to fill a void. Rather than explore the void, it had become habit to eat when I was bored rather than allow my imagination to move me out of boredom. It's easy for me to use food as a means for comfort, security and companionship.

I'm not saying that food is bad, not at all! What I've come to understand, is that the intention behind why and what we eat is important. Ayurveda has taught me this. I openly admit that I still struggle at times with my relationship to food. I still eat out of boredom or raid the fridge to avoid feeling discomfort. The difference is that I'm very aware of when I'm doing this, and because I'm aware, I am able to work through it.

Approaches I Take When Shifting My Relationship with Food

When I find that I am binge eating or making unhealthy food choices, I put myself back in check by doing these simple things:

- Praying over my food – something I suggest doing over every meal. If you haven't watched Dr. Emoto's water experiment videos I highly suggest you do.

- Mindful Eating – I sit in silence. This can be so challenging, because I usually want to scroll through my phone or watch tv while I eat. I will make myself sit in silence and without distraction while I contemplate what I'm eating, giving gratitude for all the people and effort it took to bring the meal together and on my plate - i.e. the farmers, the soil, the sun, the rain, the distributors, the vendors, the grocery store or market, and any other contributors.

- When I fall down the spiral of eating out or eating processed foods, I look up fun fresh recipes that I know will satisfy my taste buds.

- I drink more water and herbal teas.

- I make sure that I'm getting the right amount of movement and exercise. Lots of times, for me, an unhealthy relationship with food coincides with being more sedentary than active.

- I'll use EFT (Emotional Freedom Technique). Check out Brittany Watkins who does work with emotional eating!

- I make sure I'm getting enough sleep, about 8 hours a night.

These are just a few of the simple things I've found useful in shifting my relationship with food. A habit isn't something you are going to change overnight, remember that.

Ayurvedic Recipes That I Use for Nourishment and Grounding

This is a recipe I received during a cleanse. The food during an ayurvedic cleanse is so good – really, you can actually eat food. You don't have to starve yourself!

Cacao Brownie Ball Recipe

Ingredients
1 1/2 cups	Walnuts
1 1/2 cups	Medjool Dates
1/2 cup	Raw Cacao
3 dashes	Cinnamon
Pinch	Salt

*I love to add fresh coconut to mine. If you use a young coconut scoop out all the coconut flesh for the recipe. If you use a mature coconut then you only need 2-3 medium sized chunks.

Directions
Combine all ingredients into a food processor or Vitamix type blender. Blend until smooth. Scoop mixture into tablespoon sized balls. Get ready to enjoy. These really do taste like chocolate deliciousness.

Kitchari

This is a traditional ayurvedic staple, the "chicken soup" of ayurveda great for settling digestion, soothing a sick body, and is used during cleansing.

There are so many different ways to make this dish, but this is a recipe I've put together.

Ingredients

1 Cup	Mung Beans (whole or split – I prefer split)
1 Cup	Basmati Rice
2	Bay Leaves
6 Cups	Vegetable Stock/Chicken Stock (Bone Broth)
3 Tbsp	Ghee
3-4" Piece	Fresh Grated Ginger
4 Tbsp	Lemongrass Puree (or 2 Stalks of Fresh Lemon Grass)
3 Tbsp	Ground Coriander
2 Tbsp	Turmeric
1 Tbsp	Salt (or to taste)
1 Cup	Chopped Fennel (Bulb)
½ Cup	Toasted Unsweetened Coconut Flakes
1 Cup	Cilantro Chopped
To Taste	Lime

Directions

1. Soak mung beans and rinse the rice before using.
2. Heat the ghee. Add in the fresh fennel, begin sautéing, then add in ginger, coriander and turmeric. Cook for a few minutes.

3. Next, add the lemon grass (if using fresh stalks roll the stalks with a rolling pin or something of the like.) You can throw in a pinch of salt.
4. Add in the rice and mung beans coating them with the spices.
5. Add the vegetable or chicken stock and bay leaves.
6. Bring liquid to a boil then reduce the heat to low and let it simmer, covering the pot with a lid.
7. Stir occasionally to avoid rice sticking to the bottom of the pot.
8. Allow kitchari to cook for about 1-1 1/2 hours. The longer it simmers or sits the more the flavors come out.
9. When you are ready to eat you can top off your dish with cilantro, coconut and lime, to taste. I love topping this dish with lots of cilantro and lime! It brightens up the dish.

Sabrina's Herbal Spiced "Tea"

This is an herbal and spice blend I've put together that is super soothing for digestion.

Ingredients

2	Cinnamon Sticks
10	Cardamom Pods (green)
½ - 1 Tbsp	Coriander Seeds
½ - 1 Tbsp	Fennel Seeds

Directions

1. Add the above ingredients to a tea pot (if you don't own a tea pot a regular pot works fine).
2. Add 1 liter of water to the pot and bring to a boil. As soon as water comes to a boil lower the heat and bring to a simmer. Allow the ingredients to sink to the bottom of the pot.
4. If you choose to sweeten your drink, you can serve with Raw Honey, Raw Sugar (Turbinado), Raw Agave, Stevia.

Check out some more recipes, yoga and inspiration on my Pinterest page:

https://www.pinterest.com/sabrinajoatto

SABRINA JO ATTO

My Relationship to Exercise & Ayurveda

Living a sedentary lifestyle isn't a nourishing or healthy lifestyle choice. It's important to get up and move the body for at least a few minutes daily. Moving the body, whether it's through yoga, cardio, a walk, weight training, or dance helps to get the blood circulating and oxygenated, and move healthy hormones and chemicals throughout the body.

For years I hit the gym full force, pushing myself through high intensity workouts. There were times I would feel nauseous during these workouts. Instinctively I knew that wanting to throw up or faint from working out was not healthy, but I would push through anyway, because I wanted to prove I could or because I wanted to be stronger. There were times that avoiding these types of workouts like boot camps or power vinyasa classes made me feel like I was weak or lazy. When I began to understand that my fiery constitution, pitta, didn't do well with high intensity workouts and that those workouts were more likely to bring me disharmony than nourish me, it was a cathartic realization. I began to understand why workouts that were so popular didn't work for me. My body needs to move, but in a way that fans the fire within me so that it stays glowing and warm, but not to the point that the movement is throwing gasoline on the fire.

Ayurveda has not just taught me how to eat well or workout, but ultimately it has opened my eyes to areas of my life where I was pushing, controlling or falling into habits that could and did foster anxiousness.

My brief description of ayurveda doesn't begin to unravel the mysteries and goodness this ancient practice has to offer. Like I said earlier, this practice is experiential. I could list reasons, experience, and anecdotes all day regarding this holistic modality, but the power comes from you actually experiencing what it has to offer.

Here are some resources for you to explore if you are interested in learning more,

Ayurvedic Resources and Teachers I Love
- **Banyan Botanicals** www.BanyanBotanicals.com

- **Vidya Living: Ancient Wisdom for Modern Women** www.VidyaLiving.com

- **The Chopra Center** www.Chopra.com

- **Eat, Taste, Heal: An Ayurvedic Guidebook and Cookbook for Modern Living** www.EatTasteHeal.com

- **Marc Holzman** www.MarcHolzman.com, yoga practices, online ayurveda teachings and more

- **The Joyful Belly** Healthy Dieting & Digestion Made Easy with Ayurveda www.JoyfulBelly.com

- **HeyMonicaB** A Blooming Resource on Ayurveda http://heymonicab.com/

- **Karma Yoga Bloomfield Hills, Michigan** www.karma-yoga.net (If you're local to Metro Detroit, Karma yoga has an experienced team of practitioners with an incredible understanding of yoga and ayurveda.)

- **Natalie Piet** Anusara Yoga Teacher and Ayurvedic Practitioner, she offers annual workshops in Ayurveda through Karma Yoga in Bloomfield Hills, Michigan and throughout Metro Detroit.

- **Samantha Mee** Ayurvedic Counselor, offers workshops throughout Metro Detroit https://www.paramdev-kaur.com

**Yoga Pose That Has You Upside Down & Loving It
Viparita Karani or Legs Up the Wall Pose**

This is a restorative yoga pose that is incredible for resetting the nervous system. Great if you're looking to decompress before bed.

Practicing Viparita Karani
Basic Alignment Cues & Variations

1. Sit on your right side and snuggle your butt up against the wall. Your legs can be folded into your chest or extended so you're making an L shape with your body on the floor.
2. Keeping your butt flush to the wall roll onto your back taking your legs up the wall.
3. Depending on the tightness of the hamstrings you may choose to move further away from the wall to find comfort. Those with more flexibility in the hamstrings may choose to keep the butt flush to the wall.
4. Allow your arms to be at your sides relaxed with palms facing the sky.
5. Stay here for anywhere between 5-15minutes.

Pose Modifications & Variations: You can keep your back resting on the floor or take a block, blanket or bolster under the sacrum elevating the hips, helping to keep natural curve. Be sure to also keep the natural curve of the neck (not flattening it to the floor).

♥ **10** ♥

Routine & Habit

Our body likes, some might even say craves, consistency. Knowing what to expect has a settling effect, that's why we might find it's easier to stay with unhealthy habits or mindsets because we know what they bring. The drama, stress or pain is familiar and there is some comfort in that, odd as it sounds. But you're here to cultivate healthy habits, right?

One approach to settling feelings of anxiousness or chaos is to create a routine for yourself. For some, routine is naturally cathartic. They like to know their schedule and plan out their days. For others, (I'll call you my cronies) the idea of routine is suffocating. It sounds rigid and claustrophobic. Does that sound dramatic? That's probably because it is. I've learned that routine doesn't have to be suffocating or rigid. In fact, routine can be super fun, relaxing, or even energizing. There are different approaches to implementing routine. You just have to find the one that works for you.

The key to implementing this tool, like all the tools, is to meet yourself where you're at. Please don't set up unrealistic expectations for yourself in creating a routine or rituals for your day. Start small and take baby steps. A little always goes a long way.

Using Routine as a Tool for Grounding

When the mind knows where it's going, there is a sense of ease that accompanies that knowing. Because life comes with so many uncertainties, it's nice that we can carve out some time in our lives for something familiar, nourishing and personal.

You may already have a morning, afternoon, or evening routine that you follow. Some of you will be aware of these routines and others of you may not have thought of your actions as routine. For example say around 3:00 or 4:00 PM you get up from your desk at work and get yourself a snack or a coffee, maybe you walk around the office and chat it up with a coworker. Another example would be your morning cup of coffee. Maybe every night before bed you watch television.

We all get into the routine of certain habits. What I would like to offer you in this chapter is to become aware of what those habits are, and whether or not they are nourishing. Are these habits helping you to settle anxiousness or do they feed into anxiety?
For example, maybe you are someone who likes to sleep into the very last minute before having to get up. After snoozing the alarm five times you jump out of bed, frantically get ready then rush out of the house. You maybe slam a coffee and breakfast bar as you're driving to work, class, or as you take the kids to school. This routine/habit is far from nourishing. Thankfully, it doesn't take much to transform this into a routine that can be healthy.

> **Exercise:**
> **Awareness Exercise**
> Take a moment to reflect on the habits you are currently practicing.
>
> What does your morning typically look like?

What does your afternoon typically look like?

What does your evening typically look like?

NOTE: A FREE workbook containing this and all the exercises in this book is available for download from my website.

www.sabrinajoatto.com/book

Creating a Routine That's Nourishing
I'm of the belief that if we absolutely love something it becomes our medicine. With that said, I firmly believe that what we choose to be a part of our routine must be things we love. Adopting a routine that some "health guru", yoga teacher, or (fill in the blank) coach suggests isn't going to be effective unless it resonates with who you are and what you want.

For example, I love to take my time in the morning when I get up. I tend to move super slow, so packing in a bunch of self care acts into my morning routine doesn't work well for me. My routine reflects things that I find soothing, healthy and realistic.

In the afternoon, I know I hit a lull around 3:00PM. What is nourishing for me at this time is to incorporate some movement, take a walk, go to the gym, and invigorate my mind and body. Mediation isn't good for me at this time of day, as it tends to make me sleepy and unproductive. Once I incorporate some movement at this time I am recharged and ready to take on the rest of the day's work.

In the evening, after a full day of work and errands I am ready to just rest and recharge. My default is to throw myself on the couch and watch a movie, the Food Network or HGTV - I love me some Chopped or Rehab Addict. This isn't always the most nourishing routine for me though. When I get into the habit of doing this, I find myself falling asleep on the couch and not getting the most restful sleep. That's when I take account of unhealthy habits and change my pattern. Habits that nourish me in the evening are things that soothe the body - I'm on my feet all day long so getting off my feet is an incredible feeling. A hot cup of tea and some chill music on some nights is perfect. Other nights it's a good book. Some nights it is television, and other nights I hang with family or friends. My evenings are when I allow space and variety in my routine. I set a time when I'm done with work, chores, and errands. I set a time to relax - however that might look.

Practices That Could Make Up a Morning, Afternoon, & Evening Routine

- Going to the Bathroom
- Tongue Scraping
- Brushing Teeth
- Taking a Shower
- Taking a Bath
- Body Brushing
- Abhyanga (Self Massage with Warm Oil - awesome to do before a bath/shower)
- Foot Soak
- Foot Massage
- Drinking Water
- Drinking Hot Water with Lemon
- Drinking Coffee/Tea
- Praying
- Meditation
- Working Out
- Yoga

- Stretching
- Pranayama (Breathwork)
- Journaling
- Contemplation
- Reading
- Going for a Walk
- Create - writing, painting, music, scrapbooking, crocheting, drawing, etc. (Some form of artistic/creative outlet)
- Spending time with family or friends
- Spending time in nature

Creating routine in your day is your way of allowing the mind and body to be at ease. This is an opportunity for you to create practices and habits that make you happy, nourish you, provide wellness and peace of mind. An anxious mind does well with structure.

Imagine you are a balloon and anxiety is the helium that fills the balloon. The helium has the ability to take the balloon (you) for a ride! You want to keep the balloon grounded so that you don't lose it - literally and figuratively! Think of routine as the walls that keep the balloon from flying out into space. Think of the practices you choose (yoga, massage, a cup of tea while sitting in silence) as anchors that keep the balloon from bouncing around the room. Routine acts as an anchor to keep you grounded and settled.

Exercise:
Creating a Routine That Nourishes You
Make a list of things you love and want to incorporate into your day. These can include the tools and ideas that you're looking to adapt from this book.

Now, take this list and create a routine that allows for you to practice the things that make you happy.

Morning Routine
What would your ideal morning look like?

Is this currently a realistic routine? Could you incorporate this routine tomorrow?

If not how could you take baby steps to incorporate this into your morning routine?

Afternoon Routine
What would your ideal afternoon look like?

Is this currently a realistic routine? Could you incorporate this routine tomorrow?

If not how could you take baby steps to incorporate this into your morning routine?

Evening Routine
What would your ideal evening look like?

Is this currently a realistic routine? Could you incorporate this routine tomorrow?

If not how could you take baby steps to incorporate this into your morning routine?

NOTE: A FREE workbook containing this and all the exercises in this book is available for download from my website.
www.sabrinajoatto.com/book

♥ II ♥

A Different Kind of Prayer

"There is a voice that does not use words. Listen."
— Rumi

Prayer is how we communicate with the Divine. It's how we offer up our worries, concerns, challenges. It's how we give thanks and praise. Prayer is a direct line to God. I've found that praying solely for the things I want isn't as effective in reducing stress and anxiety as is praying for guidance.

Of course it's important to have visions for our life, future, health, etc. I believe that holding those visions in our hearts is important in bringing them into fruition. However, praying over and over for a specific outcome, a specific scenario isn't exercising faith. It's basically you being a broken record, telling the Big Guy you don't trust He's heard you. Praying for the same thing over and over and over again is like a nag who just won't let up and I know you don't want to be obnoxious.

So, how are we supposed to pray? Not that I think I have the answers to powerful prayers - I don't, and not to say that this is the only way to pray; but what I've found useful in reducing anxiety and making headway on the life I want is to pray for guidance. Let me explain. I love this message, "Worry not about tomorrow but pray for guidance in what you can do today." — Doreen Virtue Angel Cards. This says it all.

Praying for guidance means that rather than focusing on the outcome, you ask God what you can do today to help move you in the direction of your desired outcome.

Here are some examples of what I mean:

You want to feel calm and peaceful. Rather than asking for your stress to be taken away you could pray, "God, what would you have me learn from this situation, experience, feeling, etc.?" "What would you have me do, know, and understand to transcend this feeling of anxiety?"

This is powerful, because by asking God what you could learn, know, and understand, you are seeking to resolve the anxiety at the root. You are willing to confront the fear rather than push it away. Anxiety doesn't show up in our lives for no reason. It's there to tell us something about ourselves. We owe it to ourselves to listen and respect what it's trying to share.

You want to meet someone romantically. Rather than asking to meet a guy/girl for romantic purposes you could pray, "God, what would you have me do today to attract the perfect romantic partner for me?"

This is powerful, because by asking God, "What would you have me do?", you aren't demanding something of the Universe, you are acknowledging that you are co-creator of your life.

You are trying to figure out your career path. Rather than praying for the right career to show up or for you to force a career onto yourself you could pray, "God, what would you have me do today to help me uncover the right career for me?"

This is the same as the example above, in that by acknowledging that you are co-creator of your life and praying for guidance you are stepping up to the game. This is a major step toward initiative and confidence.

One last example,
You are having family/friend/relationship issues and don't know how to handle the situation. Rather than praying for the person or situation to change you could pray, "God, how would you have me see this differently? How would you have me see this/them?"

This is powerful, because you are acknowledging that peace starts with you. By asking how would you have me see this differently, you are open to seeing with eyes of love, compassion and forgiveness opposed to anger, resentment, and fear. Praying to see things through different eyes may not change the situation or person but it will change how you react and feel toward the situation/person.

Praying for guidance requires us to then listen for an answer. I believe it was Dianna Robinson who said, "Prayer is when you talk to God; meditation is when you listen to God." Once you pray for guidance it's important to sit in stillness; use meditation, pranayama (breathing exercises), yoga nidra, contemplation, and/or the tools given to you in this book to create opportunities for stillness and silence.

It's in that silence that the answers exist.

Praying for guidance is an opportunity to move toward your desires, one step at a time, rather than anxiously waiting for them to arrive.

WAYS TO PRAY FOR GUIDANCE

God/Father/Universe...
What would you have me know?
What would you have me do?
What would you have me say?
What would you have me learn?
How would you have me see this?
How can I see this differently?
What lessons are here for me to learn?
What steps would you have me take right now to...
What actions would you have me take today to...
What words would you have me write?

WAYS GOD OR THE UNIVERSE COULD COMMUNICATE GUIDANCE

- You may have a gut feeling or instinct about something E.g. You get the feeling to take a course at a local community house and the feeling stays with you.
- You may get a sign - something that stands out to you and makes you feel like it's a message E.g. You are looking to start your own business and you get invited to attend a seminar on starting your own business.
- You may feel the sudden urge to call or contact someone you haven't seen in a while.
- You may have a dream that shares some guidance.
- Through other people, you may be having a conversation with someone and they say something that you needed to hear or that gives you clarity.
- Ideas, thoughts, clarity come to you during or after meditation or contemplation.

These are just some ways you may be guided in response to your prayers.

Exercise:
Crafting Powerful Prayer

Think of at least one thing you may be currently praying for and write what the prayer is that you've been saying. If you don't usually pray, think of an area or situation in your life that could use some guidance and write down what that situation is.

Now, rephrase that prayer that you have been saying so that it models the examples above. Rephrase the prayer so that it aligns you with your desires or take the situation you wrote and create a prayer for guidance. e.g. "God, what would you have me do today to finish writing this book?"

NOTE: A FREE workbook containing this and all the exercises in this book is available for download from my website.

www.sabrinajoatto.com/book

SABRINA JO ATTO

♥ 12 ♥

What's the Story You've Been Telling Yourself

You may have heard or even seen a poster that reads, "You are the author of your life story." Susan Statham's spin on this adage is on point, "Your life is your story. Write well. Edit often." I love this because it recognizes that we are the co-creator of our life, and that it's important to make corrections and changes along the way.

When I first started writing this book, I was so afraid to make mistakes, to sound silly, or unorganized. I wanted each word that flowed onto the paper to be magic. I noticed that when I was stuck in that thinking that my creativity became stagnant.

I had to remind myself that I'm allowed as many rough drafts as I need, and that I have an editor and writing coach to help me along the way. She is there to help me correct the grammatical errors and connect ideas and words so that they are cohesive.

Write Well

How we choose to see a situation will directly affect our experience. Our perspective becomes our story. When I chose to see writing as something linear, "get points across, sound clear and focused, make sure not to make mistakes…" I wasn't able to think outside the box, or be creative and spontaneous. I had an idea of what I was supposed to write and I had to communicate that idea.

This perspective was so stiff, black and white that it was shutting me down in my writing. This perspective could have led to avoiding the work that needed to get done, or me deciding not to write or finish the project, and feelings of inadequacy toward writing.

The faith or love based perspective I chose to take on sounded more like this, "This is a creative process. I'm open to changing the direction of the book/the chapter. I'm okay with having horrible grammar and using words incorrectly (my editor will correct my mistakes). It's okay if this book is a dud--it's a learning experience, and I'm accomplishing something I've always dreamt of doing.
It's this loved based perspective of non-perfection and uncertainty, that has allowed me to enjoy the process of writing. My original perspective was fear based and insecure, resulting in writer's block.

My point in sharing this experience is to illustrate how the story we tell ourselves can influence how we experience life. The act of writing itself isn't what needed to change. It was how I chose to view writing, the story I told myself about writing a book, that determined what kind of experience I was going to have while working on the book.

Edit Often
When we think of daily life as an endless rough draft, a place where we can make mistakes, be messy and just let our creative juices flow without judgment, it totally takes the pressure off being perfect or good enough. When we accept that we have daily opportunities to edit, meaning reflect on the choices we make or the story we've started to write, and make changes, corrections, or redirect we take a huge load off our shoulders. It's the load or burden of not screwing up, of taking the right path, choosing the right job or school, choosing the right mate and so on.

We have the choice to write ourselves an ending that's happy. Even when things seem impossible, tragic, or finished. We can bring joy to our story by changing the perspective, the narrator's (your) voice. You have the opportunity to make the main character a hero rather than a victim.

Here are two examples of the same story told from two different perspectives: a main character who's a victim and a main character who's the hero.

Synopsis:
Erika has been dating a great guy for the last two months. He's looking to take the relationship to the next level and she's feeling a bit of pressure to move forward or end things. Erika is working on being more vulnerable, communicating her feelings and expressing emotions that would otherwise make her feel uncomfortable or too open. At the same time, she's noticing qualities and characteristics that she might consider deal breakers. Erika is feeling a bit of anxiety over the situation. She isn't sure what direction to move this relationship.

Erika's Anxiety Perspective/ The Victim
"I'm dating a guy who I like but I'm not sure how much I like him. I feel pressured to be vulnerable and open and that's making me want to run away. This guy's expectations for the relationship are making me feel like I should be more into the relationship. Part of me, the part that feels pressured, wants to end things. Then there's a part of me that wants to give this a little more time. With all this uncertainty I'm focusing on the "what ifs", trying to control the outcome. And if I can't control the outcome, then I want to know it so I can control how things will go down before the outcome. I'm so frustrated, I don't know what the right direction is!"

With all that fear and need for control, Erika is feeling major anxiety. Her feelings seem jumbled up and unclear. She's more likely to act out in ways that are unhealthy due to frustration than react in a way that creates clarity and grounding.

Here is how she chose to edit the story she's been replaying in her mind and become the hero of her situation rather than the victim.

Rewrite - Erika's Love Perspective

"I'm in a relationship with a really great guy, who I know I like as a friend and possibly more. My feelings are going in and out and this confuses me. I'm glad to be dating a man who shows me affection and is caring and loving. Seeing these qualities in a guy I'm dating lets me know that this is something I want and deserve. I've noticed he needs some reassurance from me that the relationship is going in the direction he wants and I'm not sure I can give him that assurance. What I can do is be honest.
I can express how I'm feeling in a way that's real and kind. Just because he's all in and I'm not doesn't mean that I need to be all in right now. All I can do is work with what I have, and today all I have are my honest feelings. Whether things progress with our relationship or end, this has been and will be a great opportunity for me to grow and learn about myself and what I need and want in a relationship."

This love perspective, is a voice of empowerment. Erika is the hero rather than the victim. Her rhetoric is hopeful, clear and strong. She's writing herself an ending that leaves her on top. She is reacting to her situation with confidence and power.
It's in recognizing that we have the ability to write our story and change that story at any moment by simply changing our perspective that moves us from anxiety and fearful living to a peaceful mind and peace filled life.

Tips for Editing

Rhetoric Patterns Heard from a Victim
They make me feel...
I don't have a choice...
He/She did/said/was _____ to me...
I feel pressured...
Life is so hard...
Why do I always get the shit end of the deal?...
I always get burned/screwed/taken advantage of...
Life sucks...
I'm unlucky/I don't have good luck...
Good things don't happen to me/for me...
I wish I could be like _____, but that's just not in my card...
I'm not smart enough...
I'm not pretty enough...
I'm not cool enough...
I don't have the same opportunities successful people do...
I'm not meant for greatness...
It's not my fault, if _____ would just _____ then
I should do this/that...

You get the picture, this type of dialogue or thinking is victim mentality. This type of thinking will only hinder you from success, happiness and peace of mind.

Rhetoric Patterns Heard from a Hero
This experience/ situation is an opportunity for growth...
No one can make me feel inferior without my permission...
I have the choice to...
I could do this/that... (could over should creates options rather than punish)

All I can do is be where I'm at and work with what I have and that's enough...

I'm enough...

What I have and who I am right now is good enough...

If I'm brought to it I'm ready for it...

Mistakes are opportunities for growth and stepping stones to success...

My mistakes are gifts...

Those who challenge me are my greatest teachers...

This type of dialogue and thinking empowers you. It puts joy and peace into your hands and not in the hands of others or other external factors.

What is the story you've currently been telling yourself? Write it out.

Then edit that story, making the main character (you) a hero.

♥ 13 ♥

Stepping Into Fear

"What we resist persists," I remember hearing that and a light bulb going off in my mind. When and if we choose to resist a situation, experience or thought it will continue to make itself present and known; it will persist. What I've come to understand about anxiety and the thoughts or ideas that bring about our anxiety is that if we choose to resist those thoughts or ideas, if we choose to deny they exist or to run away from them, they will become more and more intense. The more you try to shut out anxiety the louder it becomes.

What I have found healing was rather than trying to rid myself of anxiousness and rather than breathe it away or think it away, I've allowed myself to sit with the feeling. Now, this doesn't mean I didn't use the tools in this book to help bring grounding or a settled feeling in the physical body. I did. However, I also chose to listen to what my anxiety wanted to tell me.

What it Means to Sit with Your Anxiety

The way you would sit with a friend who is scared and upset is the same way I want you to treat your anxiety. If a friend comes to you with a sadness or fear and they are spilling their guts, as a compassionate listener, you would silently hear what they have to say without judgment and with an open heart. When you're healing anxiety it is important that you become that incredible, loving, compassionate and non-judgmental friend to yourself. You are being called to look deeply at the areas of your inner self that require love.

I typically use this analogy to explain the love approach...
Think of anxiety as a bully. You have two approaches when confronted with a bully. Typically, bullies want to push your buttons, trigger anger, fear, and unsettling feelings. They want to feel powerful and dominant, right? What are your options?

1. You could push back, fight, argue or resist, but what that does is offer an opportunity for the bully to keep pushing your buttons and antagonizing you. Replace the bully with your anxiousness of, let's say, commitment. You find yourself stressing about committing to a job or about a project. Your initial response is to want to push the negative responses to anxiety away. You try pushing away the tightness in your chest, the knot in your stomach, the feeling of uneasiness that are all coming up for you. However, the more you try to push these reactions away, the more you try to ignore the feelings that are coming up, the more they will persist. Because like a bully, the anxiety wants attention. The more you ignore it the louder it becomes.

2. What if you listened to the bully? You let her say all the negative, mean, damning comments she could throw your way. What if you recognized that you could listen to everything this bully was saying and not take it personally. What if you gave the bully attention, acknowledgment and

respect. You show this bully that you're not intimidated.

How would she respond? Most likely she would find someone else she knew she could intimidate. This second approach is learning to sit with your anxiety. How do you do this?

How to Sit With The Anxiety

Your anxiety, say over commitment, creeps up on you. You feel the knot in your stomach, tightness in your chest, and begin the cycle of negative self talk and limiting beliefs. Instead of trying to push these feelings away, and ignore that they are there, you take the time to acknowledge said feelings. That bully voice of anxiety starts to quiet down. Anxiety starts to dissipate. Why? Because the emotional and physiological responses we have to anxiety are messages for us to become aware. If we choose to ignore those messages they won't stop coming in, they only get louder and louder until we can no longer ignore them.

And sometimes the longer we wait the more challenging the lesson becomes. Anxiety, like any other experience we have, is an opportunity for growth. It's a chance to move away from darkness and into the light of peace.

Steps for Sitting With Anxiety

When anxiousness becomes apparent, meaning you feel physical or emotional discomfort.

1. Acknowledge these feelings by stating the obvious. For example: my chest is tight, my heart is beating fast/irregular, I'm terrified, I'm being stubborn and inflexible, I feel frozen, I feel jittery.

2. Pay attention to your thoughts. What is it that you are telling yourself or have been telling yourself about the situation? For example: "I'm not good enough to get this done." "I'm not pretty enough to keep this guy around." "I don't make enough money to pay the bills." "I hate my job but I need to make money." "If I don't do this then something bad might happen." "A good person does _____ , but I don't want to do that." "I don't have enough time to do what I want or need." (The list could go on forever!)

3. Contemplate these feeling and thoughts. Objectively look at them, and understand that anything true/real wouldn't bring about fear.

4. Ask God to help you see the situation differently. This short prayer can be worded any way that feels authentic and comfortable for you. I usually say, "God, help me to see this differently. Help me to see this through your eyes."

5. Repeat this any time anxiety or stress creeps up on you.

Like with everything I've shared in this book the best results come with consistency. The more you practice something, the stronger you will experience its effects.

In step 3, I suggest that you contemplate the feelings that are coming up. The purpose in doing this is to begin to recognize patterns, ideas, or belief systems that may be contributing to your anxiety. Once you have a clearer idea of these ideologies then you can sort through them. Where did you pick up or learn these fear based ideologies? What purpose do you have for holding on to them? Why and how do you identify with these beliefs? Are you willing to move away from the limiting beliefs that are fostering anxiety? If not, why?

Take a moment to note down some answers to these questions.

Asking yourself these deep and revealing questions can be vulnerable and challenging for some of us. Whether you find it easy to delve deep or it's more of a chore, know that these questions will be waiting for you today, or whenever you choose to ask them, and hear the answers. The more clear we get about our anxiety the less scary it appears, and this is when the anxiety starts to dissolve.

Let's Revisit an Analogy to Make the Point...

You enter a room that is dark and you can't see clearly. You start to make out shapes but that's about it. In the corner of the room you see a distorted figure and it completely freaks you out. Your mind begins to run wild with ideas of what this distorted figure is. You create a monster, a threat in your mind. Instead of running away you decide that you are going to confront the "monster". At first, the closer you get the higher your anxiety becomes. Your heart races, threatening thoughts fill your mind, your palms sweat and all you want to do is retreat and avoid this horrible hideous "thing". Then something begins to shift, because you persevere, slowly your anxiety begins to lessen. You begin to see the object a little more clearly with each step. Eventually you get to the figure and there is a lamp next to it, you turn the lamp on and you see that the figure was a teddy bear.

I know this analogy is cliché, but it's cliche for a reason, and that's because it makes the point well. Many times what we fear is nothing more than a figment of our imagination. We've taken something that's there but distorted it to a point of unreality. It's simply not there. We've made it up out of the pain of the feeling of anxiety.

Any real "threat" comes with a sense of calm, grounding, and centeredness. We move into action mode, and self preservation kicks in. If there was REALLY a monster in the room, you'd instinctively know how to protect yourself.

♥ 14 ♥

Forgiveness

"Fear binds the world. Forgiveness sets it free."

— A Course in Miracles

Forgiveness is one of the most important avenues to transcending anxiety and living with peace. Forgiveness has the power to release heavy feelings of suffering you may or may not realize you are carrying.

I've heard people say:

"Why should I forgive?"

"That person or situation doesn't deserve my forgiveness." "They hurt me and I want them to hurt."

"They're dead to me."

These thoughts, ideas and words are very damaging to the person saying them and feeling them. They reflect the fear that I spoke about in chapter one. They foster darkness in our hearts and blind us from the light that will bring about peace.

If you are reading this book it's because you are seeking peace;

peace of mind, peace in your heart, peace in your life, and it is through forgiveness that you will obtain peace.

Why Forgiveness Brings Peace

Forgiveness is an acceptance of Love. When we choose to forgive we have chosen to look past our expectations of people, life, and circumstance and see instead opportunity for growth, divinity, and purpose. It is through our ability to love unconditionally that brings healing. An act of fear, like: hate, anger, or manipulation, is only healed when the opposite is made present. That opposite is love, meaning: non-judgment, patience, and respect. When Love is present peace is present.

Understanding Forgiveness

Forgiveness is shifting your perspective from fear to love, just as we spoke about earlier in this book. Forgiveness is an opportunity to shift perspective from blaming or shaming to one of compassion and understanding. Forgiveness does not see the deceit, violence, abuse, or ill will that has been acted out. Forgiveness sees the fear behind the act. Forgiveness offers love where love has been forgotten.

Not Confusing Acceptance or Justification with Forgiveness

I think it's easy for us to assume we have forgiven someone or a situation because we have accepted the situation for what it is, or a person for who they are. Acceptance doesn't mean we have actually forgiven the situation or person. The same goes for justifying a situation. It might be easy to justify why someone is abusive, cheats, or lies. We often accept or justify their actions, because we don't want to lose the relationship or it's easier to sweep the issue under the rug. Understand that acceptance and justification do not transform feelings of hurt, pain, resentment, or fear.

Even though you have accepted something or someone, you can still be feeling emotions of anger, resentment, and hurt. It isn't until those feelings of hurt are replaced with love that forgiveness has taken place.

What Forgiveness Feels Like

You know you have truly forgiven and let love into your heart when you can reflect on a situation that once brought you pain and you no longer feel fear, victimization, or anger. *Instead you reflect on the situation and there is peace that follows.* You don't have a knot in your stomach, you don't feel tense or stiff, you don't feel sick thinking about the situation. *You feel calm, centered, and at ease.* You know you have forgiven a person when you no longer feel the need to tell them off, avoid them, cringe at the sight of them, or feel the need to get back at them. *You have forgiven them when you can be in their presence and experience calm, ease, and comfort regardless of your history with them.*

How to Move Toward Forgiveness

Forgiveness is a process. It may not be something that you are going to come to overnight. Moving toward forgiveness requires you to practice all the principles we've talked about in this book. You can use the steps below to help you begin moving toward forgiveness and peace. Reread and reflect on the chapters to help you get clear.

Think of a person or situation in your life that requires your forgiveness. (The person can even be you. I think it is safe to say that all humans need to learn to forgive themselves for the big and little guilt we put on ourselves.)

Love vs. Fear

Once you have the person or situation to forgive in mind, become aware of your thoughts and emotional patterns. Where do your thoughts flow? What are you feeling? Remember chapter one's list of fear and love based thinking. Make a list of what's going on in your mind and heart. Then distinguish if it falls under love or fear. After recognizing your fear based thoughts, note how you can shift your thinking to love based thoughts.

Intention (Sankalpa)

A sankalpa is a resolve. What are you resolving to forgive? What seeds are you choosing to plant?

Having Faith

Take a look at the list you just made. Remind yourself that by planting seeds of love, you will in time, harvest peace and ease. Keep in mind that most likely you are going to experience resistance while doing this exercise. That resistance is fear, and it's fine to feel that way. This is where faith plays a role. Know that in time that resistance will soften and eventually go away.

Surrender & Stepping Into Fear

When resistance shows up, take a really close look at it and recognize it for what it is, fear. Allow yourself to sit with it. What does it want to show you? What does it have to say? Surrendering is like telling fear, "I don't want to fight," and once you give up the fight, well there is no reason for the other party to attack. You start to see the vulnerability in fear. You begin to notice that it doesn't have a hold on you and that it can't hurt you.

Being Where You Are & Practicing Kindness

Be conscious of not judging yourself for feeling the way you do. It isn't wrong to feel hurt, sad or angry. However, it's holding on to those emotions that can cause you suffering. Remember, "The journey of a thousand miles begins with a single step," Lao- Tzu. Allow yourself time to move through the process of forgiveness.

Imagine you have spent years trapped in a house that was dark. And over those years you adjusted your sight to the darkness. If you were to open your front door, after years of darkness and step out into the bright light you would find your eyes tearing up and burning. The light is so intense.

In order to survive in the dark, you had to adjust to the dark. Living in the light is to see from a different perspective and to move from dark to light we must slowly adjust.

Moving from fear to love is very similar. Instead of walking out of the house after years of no light, you must first crack the shades that are covering the windows. You start by cracking open one window shade. Then once you've adjusted to that amount of light you begin to open the shades of that window fully over time. Then you start to open the shades of the other windows in the house. Eventually the entire house is full of light.

Once you've adjusted to the house being full of light, you can walk outside and comfortably see. You don't experience discomfort from the brightness.

This is similar to the process of forgiveness. When we hold on to fear we learn to adjust to darkness. When it's time for us to exercise love and move into the light, it can be very uncomfortable. We want to resist the experience, close our eyes and shut out the brightness.

Being where you are is an exercise in adjusting to the light by being patient and allowing the process to take place slowly and naturally.

We, Not Me & Being of Service

Forgiveness becomes easier when you recognize that you don't have to go about it alone. You have Divine support that you can lean on. It also becomes easier when you recognize that your forgiveness serves a higher purpose.

Choosing forgiveness is the greatest and fastest way for us to contribute to the healing of the world. We have two choices, we can add to the chaos by holding onto fear or we can aid in healing by exercising love. Our service and purpose in this life is to promote healing.

What's the Story You've Been Telling Yourself?

Listen to your story. Are you the hero or the victim? Are you asking for direction or are you wallowing in self pity? If your story makes you a victim then rewrite it, and if you don't know how to rewrite it ask for guidance.

A Different Kind of Prayer

Ask the Divine, as you understand it to be, "What would you have me learn from this situation?" "What would you have me learn from this person?" "What would you have me learn from this hurt or sadness?" "What would you have me do with this lesson?"

"What would you have me understand to be the hero of my story?" Ask for direction. Divinity will always transcend you.

Exercise:

Taking the time to reflect and write out the above steps will help you to plant those seeds of love and nourish them. With care, nourishment and perseverance you will move toward forgiveness and experience the bliss of peace.

NOTE: A FREE workbook containing this and all the exercises in this book is available for download from my website.

www.sabrinajoatto.com/book

Resources for Learning More about Forgiveness

Twelve Principles of Forgiveness, Jack Kornfield

A Course in Miracles, Foundation of Inner Peace

A Return to Love, Marianne Williamson

Finding Your –Ing, Gabrielle Bernstein

♥ 15 ♥

Disconnect

I'm just going to say it...Put the f@#!ing phone down! (If you couldn't tell, I mean that with so much love!) You either just silently agreed by shaking your head yes, or you felt a huge knot form in your gut and the desire to resist what you just read. "I'm NOT disconnecting!" I promise that what I'm suggesting isn't sadistic. Hear me out.

Burn Out

A good number of tools in this book are about unplugging and resetting. Have you ever noticed that when technology gets wonky, like your phone or computer freezes, the television acts up, or your iPad doesn't want to work that the solution usually is to turn it off, wait and then re-start it. When our phones, tablets, and other electronics are constantly "plugged in/running" they eventually get tired and burn out. Even they need a chance to rest in order to function properly.

If you are always "plugged in," you too will experience burn out. Give yourself that needed time to reset by turning off your device, putting it on silent, or leaving it in a place away from you. If this is a challenging exercise start by putting it away for a few minutes at a time, then slowly extend the time that you are away.

Disconnecting from what's going on around you, like the news, gossip, and peoples' drama can be very cathartic. Try it, I dare you!

Awareness Exercise: Ask yourself these questions,

> Are you glued to your devices? (i.e. phone, tablet, computer)

> If one of your devices was to break would you feel like the world just ended?

> Can you walk away from your phone (and all devices that connect to your phone) for an extended period of time and not feel anxious without it?

> If you find you are dependent on your devices I'm going to suggest you start to wean yourself off the device!

NOTE: A FREE workbook containing this and all the exercises in this book is available for download from my website.

www.sabrinajoatto.com/book

How to Wean Yourself off Device Dependency

1. Start with a reasonable amount of time to be away from all devices. Maybe it's 5 minutes, 30 minutes, 5 hours. If you have a job that requires you to be on your phone or computer most of the day then set aside time when you are not working to disconnect.

2. If you find yourself saying, "I need to keep my phone by me in case of an emergency." "I can't miss a call from a client I need the phone available 24-7." "I need to stay connected and in touch or something bad might happen." I promise you, that none of those excuses are true.

There was a time, not that long ago, when cell phones didn't exist. There was a time when phones didn't have internet connection. Guess what, people survived. People waited to hear back from someone. They didn't worry about being connected constantly. They went about their day and all was well.

I know what it's like to get caught up in the instant gratification of googling the answer, texting a friend back right away, ordering my groceries via an app. Convenience is great and I'm not telling you to write it off, I am suggesting you disconnect for short periods of time.

3. As time goes on and you slowly take longer breaks from your devices notice how you feel.

Social Media

I don't think social media is bad and I don't think that you need to erase it from your life (unless you want to). Personally, I like being able to connect with people I would normally not be connected to because of distance or other circumstance. But there are things to be aware of.

Things I've Noticed Regarding Social Media

1. **It is seriously easy to look at people's Facebook, Instagram, or Snapchat feed and think,** "Wow, they have such a cool life." "I wish my life was that great." "He/She is so attractive, why don't my selfies look like that?" Reality check! Most people only post fun pictures and moments. They take a hundred selfies before they find one that looks flawless and even then, there is an app that can hide and erase most blemishes! Their life isn't better or greater than yours.

2. **We use social media (our phones in general) as an outlet to avoid.** It's easy to become engrossed with what's going on in other people's lives, what's going on with the celebrities, and politicians rather than focusing on your life. Taking a good look at where you can grow, mentally and spiritually.

3. **Be careful of "news items" designed to scare you.** Usually, the catchiest headlines and stories are the ones that are dramatic. Sadly, this drama can be taken too far and it provokes fear when fear isn't necessary. We live in a society where everyone has become the media because of social media. Like all things this has pros and cons. Try following social accounts that are uplifting and focused on growth, love and unity rather than ratings, fear and divide.

4. **Be aware that much is not real or true.** Items about health for example. This goes along with the last statement. The internet has

a slew of information and a lot of that
information isn't accurate. If you find that
what you're reading is causing anxiety or any
kind of fear be aware that it may not be true. I
mentioned earlier that intuition comes with a
sense of peace even when its warning us of
something. Fear isn't the same as intuition.

5. **Gossip is toxic.** I get it, we all have an
opinion and we want to vocalize that opinion.
We want to be heard damn it! Hell, I'm one of
the most opinionated people I know. But the
truth is an opinion and gossip aren't the same.
Gossip is talking about others with judgment. I
bring this up not to be preachy but because
this book is meant to guide you to transcend
anxiety, meaning fear. Gossip is just another
form of fear. Remember there are two types of
thoughts fear and love. I think we can both
agree gossip isn't love.

6. **Don't engage in comment thread
arguments.** WOW! This one blows my mind
every time. The hateful words that people
throw around, the passive aggressive
commentary. Maybe you see a controversial
post or you see a post you don't care for and
you consider: "giving your opinion", "schooling
someone", or "stating the truth", this is nothing
more than drama!
Guess what, no one really cares what our
opinion is, unless we want to compliment them
and even then, so many people have a hard
time accepting that. You want to transform
anxiety? Steer clear of drama don't engage and
don't start.

7. **Notice that political arguments are completely polarized and useless. Does it make you feel better or worse to engage in it?** This builds on the last statement. Remember the intention of this work is to transform worry and fear. Be aware of the conversations you are having and how they make you feel.

Everyone is entitled to a perspective without judgment; you and others. Are your political discussions informative? Do they help you see another perspective or understand another's perspective, even if you don't agree? Healthy conversations around politics (and religion for that matter) are objective and open minded. If this can't happen between both parties, maybe you choose not to engage.

8. **Imagine being in a sudden hail storm. That's social media. It's a BARRAGE of information. Is this helpful to your anxiety?** If you feel like logging into Facebook is overstimulating, then you have the power and control to log off. Do it!

9. **Unfollow anyone/anything that isn't serving your growth.** If you find that certain accounts bring you discomfort, you have the control to unfollow those accounts. There is absolutely nothing wrong with unfollowing an account, even a friend or family member, if your emotional health is being affected. Know the difference between unfollowing an account that brings unrest and unfollowing to stir drama and make a point. All decisions we are looking to make are rooted in love. Is your

decision based out of love or fear (anger, frustration, spite)?

10. **LIMIT your time on Social Media.** Live in the real world. Look up and notice what's going on around you. You might be surprised that the answer to your prayers, healing, or a solution is sitting right in front of you. But how would you know when your face is buried in your phone? The universe is always talking to us, guiding us along our journey but we have to be present and aware to hear the conversation that the universe is looking to have with us.

Exercise:

When healing fear it's important to notice all areas that bring up anxiety for you. Does scrolling through social media make you feel anxious or less than wonderful? If you feel like you've been sucked into the lies your ego is telling you as you scroll your social media feeds, try this:

Disconnect from social media for an entire week. If this is hard for you then start slowly by disconnecting for a day, then taking time to disconnect for two days, etc. until you get to the point where you are comfortable with disconnecting for a full week.

If it is simply habit to hit the snapchat app then delete it from your phone. In fact, delete all your social apps from the phone until you are ready to get back on them. This will make it easier for you to break the habit of jumping on when you're bored.

After just a couple days of this social detox recognize how you feel? Do you feel lighter, calmer, happier? Do you feel like you're out of the loop, suffering from FOMO? Did you almost forget that FB exists? Check in and contemplate on what you're feeling.

NOTE: A FREE workbook containing this and all the exercises in this book is available for download from my website.

www.sabrinajoatto.com/book

❤ Conclusion ❤

My want for you after reading this book is to recognize that you are not alone in feeling frustrated, worried, or over whelmed and that there is a way of living that is way easier and more peaceful. Self care and self help are not to be thought of once and then forgotten. The ideas and resources you've learned or maybe been reminded of are tools that need to be returned to and exercised regularly. My suggestion is to skim through the book every few months and reread any notes you may have taken. Come back to this information and refresh the mind.

Gentle reminders are appropriate for fostering your perception of love.
Stress, chaos, uncertainty—these are all things that are out of our control. How we react to them however, is completely in our control. When you utilize these practices with consistency, you will begin to experience peace in the midst of stressors.

You have everything you need to feel free, vibrant, confident, and relaxed. Life is full of perfect moments. All you need to do is uncover them. The ideas and resources in this book are meant to do exactly that — help you uncover moments of peace, joy, ease, and happiness.

♥ Appendix ♥

Affirmations

Affirmations...or Incantations (Thank you Tony Robbins)

Affirmations are a tool/technique for working with the way we speak to ourselves, others, and nature. As I shared in the first chapter, the first lesson I learned was that my thoughts were very powerful.

Changing the way we speak to ourselves can have profound effects not only on how we feel but our overall experience of life.

Rather than giving you a list of generic affirmations I want to share with you some authors who have incredible knowledge and information to share about changing your thought patterns.

Louise Hay **www.louisehay.com**
Founder of Hay House Publishing and Author of numerous self-help and spiritual books, Louise Hay is queen of affirmations. She even has some cool apps you can download for your smartphone/tablet. The book *You Can Heal Your Life* changed my life!

Florence Scovel Schinn **www.florence-scovel-shinn.com/**
Author of a great number of books, Florence who lived from 1871-1940 was an artist turned spiritual teacher and metaphysical author. One of my favorite books of her's is *The Game of Life and How to Play it*.

Anthony Robbins **www.tonyrobbins.com**
I **LOVE** this guy. Tony Robbins is a motivational speaker who is known for teaching people how to empower their lives by changing patterns. I couldn't agree with his ideas and methods more! However, Tony has a bit different perspective on affirmations than others might. Check out his youtube video on Incantations vs. Affirmations
https://www.youtube.com/watch?v=l-QkhcYf4Sg

Of course, there are many other resources out there about affirmations and changing thought patterns, but I find that these three sources are incredible and will lead you further down the path toward the next teachers and tools.

❤ Appendix ❤

CONTEMPLATION

Contemplation is a reflection process. It's a time for introspection, a remembering process if you will. Some of my favorite places to contemplate are in nature or a quiet space in my home sitting on my favorite chair.

Preparing for Contemplation

1. Have a journal and pen to record your thoughts, insights, feelings, or memories.
2. Choose a time when you can be alone without interruption and without obligations.

Contemplation Process

1. Pick something that you will focus on; an area of the self that you are willing and ready to reflect upon (e.g. attachment, dependency, self-esteem, anger).
2. Sit comfortably in a chair, on the floor, or wherever you most feel comfortable. Relax the body and mind, and breathe out any tension.
3. Remember to breathe. If you find you are holding your breath, just casually come back to your natural breath. Put your attention on the idea, memory or person that you have decided to contemplate.

4. Staying connected to your breath, bring awareness to sensations, feelings, and beliefs you have regarding your topic of contemplation.
5. Allow the face and eyes to soften. Continue to release any tension that comes up.
6. Staying connected to your breath, become aware of images, ideas, feelings, memories, etc. that come up, while releasing any judgment that might surface.
7. Record what arose for you in your journal.

I hope you find this a useful tool. Enjoy the path to exploration, discovery, and awakening.

♥ Appendix ♥

Pranayama - Breath Work

Pranayama is sanskrit for breath work. There are a number of different breathing exercises in the yogic tradition, each with a specific agenda. Below I have shared with you two exercises that are specific to reducing tension, relaxing the nervous system and reducing anxiety.

3 Part Breath
Dirga Pranayama

1. Find a comfortable seat or come to lying on your back.
2. Close your eyes or soften your gaze (Soften the gaze means to release tension from the eyes. Try taking the eyes back - inward toward skull, rather than keeping them focused and intense, open your peripheral vision.)
3. Take your hands just under your navel and allow them to rest on your lower belly.
4. Begin to take an inhale through the nose and feel the belly expand and grow under your hands.
5. As you exhale feel the lower belly contract and draw in.
6. Sit for a few moments with awareness of the breath and sensations.

7. Then take your hands to your lower ribs, with each inhale feel the ribs grow and expand under your hands.

8. As you exhale feel the lower ribs contract and draw inward.

9. Sit now with awareness of the breath and sensations.

10. Next, bring your hands to the collarbone. With each inhale feel the collarbone lift. (If you don't feel the chest or collarbone lifting imagine it on each inhale).

11. On the exhale feel the chest/collarbone lower.

12. Sit for a few moments with awareness.

13. Staying connected to the breath, on an inhale, feel the lower belly, then ribs, then chest fill with air and as you exhale feel the chest, ribs, and belly deflate.

14. Sit now with awareness of the wave like breath.

Practicing this daily, if even for a couple of minutes, is an awesome exercise for getting in touch with full steady breathing, and can help you reduce or relieve your anxiety.

Alternate Nostril Breathing
(Nadi Shodhana Pranayama)

1. Sit comfortably somewhere without interruption for at least 10 minutes.

2. Keep your back straight, neck and shoulders relaxed.

3. Set up hand positioning or Mudra: curl your index and middle finger into the palm, using the thumb to close off the right nostril and the ring and pinky finger to close off the left nostril. Only one nostril will be closed at a

time. Modification: If that is challenging, hold the index and middle finger on the brow line and use the thumb to close the right nostril and the pinky and ring finger to close off the left.

4. Gently press the right nostril closed with the thumb and gently exhale out the left nostril.

5. Now, breathe in through the left nostril and at end of inhale press left nostril shut with the ring and pinky finger.

6. Remove thumb from right nostril and exhale through the right nostril.

7. Now inhale through right nostril and at the end of the inhale gently press the right nostril with your thumb.

8. Exhale through the left nostril, now inhale through the left nostril.

9. Continue this cycle of alternate nostril breathing. Start by breathing like this for 3 minutes and gradually work your way up to 10 minutes.

Tips:
• Breathe in from the same nostril that you exhaled
• Keep eyes closed
• Take relaxed breaths
• Spend a few minutes in silence after doing this breathing exercise
• Begin with an inhale through the left nostril and end with an exhale on the left nostril. The left side of the body, according to yoga and Ayurveda is linked to the parasympathetic nervous system and this is the rest and restore system aspect of the nervous system.

Traditional Mudra

Alternative Hand Gesture

❤ Appendix ❤

Yoga Asana

Asana is the physical practice of yoga. It's what most of the world associates with yoga, which is funny because it makes up such a small part of what yoga actually is. But I believe it is an important aspect of yoga, especially in a culture where we are prone to sitting behind computers, televisions and phones. (Crazy that our phones make the list.) Moving the body is super important. Asana is an opportunity to oxygenate the blood, detoxify the body, improve immunity and digestion, and so much more.

A teacher reminded me recently that we practice yoga asana because we are looking to intentionally "stress" the body. In other words, we subject the body to postures that require effort and sometimes hard work. Engaging in "stressful" situations on the mat reminds us to take action with ease, to move with mindfulness and intention. Yoga reminds us to breathe as we move. All these healthy habits can be taken off the yoga mat/class and into the real world. When you consistently practice breathing through a challenging pose in yoga, that habit starts to spill over into your work life, family life, and personal life. Yoga asana is a beautiful practice for not just getting physically healthy, but for creating habits that lead to peace.

Yoga asana is meant to bring harmony to mind, body, and spirit.

I want to clarify something about starting a yoga practice. Yoga is not meant to be a sport that pushes you to sweat and contort your body into pretzel shapes. You don't ever have to do a headstand or handstand - ever! Unless you want to. Picking up a yoga practice is about meeting your body and it's needs where you are. Starting a slow and mellow practice, especially if you're new to yoga is smart. In fact, slow and mellow may be all you ever need and want.

If you enjoy a more active style of yoga that's fine as well, but remember to be careful and to listen to your body. Self care is important and essential to healing and bringing peace to the body and mind.

Resources for an at Home Practice

Yoga with Adriene **yogawithadriene.com**
Adriene has a great library of videos that can be practiced by a yoga rookie or novice. She's also super funny! Check out her youtube channel youtube.com/yogawithadriene. She offers free videos on her youtube channel and more options for videos as member to her online yoga community.

YogaGlo **www.yogaglo.com**
This is an online market place where you can find some awesome yoga classes by incredible teachers. Yogaglo offers a ton of different yoga and meditation styles. With styles ranging from vinyasa, to restorative, to kundalini, yogaglo gives you great variety.

❤ Appendix ❤

Yoga Nidra

Nidra in sanskrit is sleep, so yoga nidra literally translates to yoga sleep. However, while practicing yoga nidra, the intention is to stay awake and not fall asleep. (Huh?)

Yoga Nidra is a tool that is meant to bring deep relaxation to the body through intentional awareness.

I went through a training called Mindful Yoga Therapy. The training was focused on working with veterans experiencing post traumatic stress. One of the things I learned in this training was how powerful yoga nidra had been for the vets who practiced it. Veterans who originally came to these yoga sessions plagued with insomnia had finally found a resource that helped them, with consistent use, to settle the nervous system and mind so they could begin getting some sleep.

I bring this up because if the practice of yoga nidra is powerful enough to bring some sense of ease to a veteran who has been through war or worse, imagine how it can benefit you.

How it works

You begin by laying on your back, taking savasana. Allowing yourself time to settle in and relax. Once settled you will listen to the instructor guide you through an awareness meditation.

By keeping awareness on what the teacher is guiding you through, you allow the brain to settle and become focused. By keeping with this focused awareness you create an opportunity for relaxed sleep to take place. Again, in yoga nidra you don't actually sleep, but this relaxed state is measurable to a deep relaxed sleep.

"When we practice yoga nidra, we are trying to transcend the behavior of the external mind" Yoga Nidra, Swami Satyananda Saraswati.

Resources
The link below will take you to a recording of Yoga Nidra that you can do at home.

www.sabrinajoatto.com/book

♥ Appendix ♥

Meditation

The word meditation alone can be intimidating and grandiose. I think a good number of us have developed, at some point or another, a silly notion that only very accomplished people or very developed people can meditate, and that if you do meditate then you are a part of a privileged few.

I'm here to debunk that notion. If you want my perspective, (you're going to get it even if you don't want it) meditation is made out to be something it is not. There are a number of different styles and methods for meditating. Based on my experience and what I've learned, here is what I understand meditation to be and not to be:

What meditation is:
- An opportunity to sit in stillness - even if stillness doesn't seem like it's coming (I'll explain this more)
- An opportunity to connect with spirit
- An opportunity to reconnect with yourself
- A sacred space

What meditation isn't:
- Sitting completely still, never moving
- Completely clearing the mind - having no thoughts
- Something that is mastered or perfected

The list of meditation styles out there is long, and depending on your culture or background, you may be more inclined to one over another. Below is a short list of different styles of meditation.

Types of Meditation:

Guided Meditation
Walking Meditation
The Rosary – A Catholic tool for meditation
Focused Attention Meditation – Use of Mantra, Sound, Breath, etc.
Open Monitoring Meditation - Non-Directive Style

If you feel that meditating is a tool you are interested in using but not sure where or how to start my suggestion is to start small.

- Begin with 3-5 minutes in the morning.
- You can do this while you wait for your morning coffee to brew, or first thing as you sit up in bed.
- Find a time and space that will allow you to follow through.
- Once you've established a morning practice add an evening practice of 3-5 minutes. You can do this right before you go to bed. (I've been told you don't want to meditate before bed because it can give you a jolt of energy but I've never had a problem. Experiment and see what works for you.)
- Once you have an established morning and evening routine that is consistent, you can think about adding time onto each session.
- I believe it's important to say a blessing or prayer before your meditation.

- Remember We not Me? Doing this helps me to make the "We" more integrated into all the other things I do throughout my day. It fosters the habit of connecting to spirit.
This could consist of "I call in God, the Angels of my Highest Good, the Holy Spirit, Ascended Masters, Love and Light" (However you choose to call in a Higher Power). Calling in a higher spirit ensures healing and divine guidance throughout the meditation.

Try this Grounding Meditation

Sit comfortably in a chair or on the floor. Sit somewhere you will not be disturbed and you will be comfortable for at least 10 minutes.

Take 3 deep cleansing breaths inhaling through the nose and exhaling through the mouth.

If you are sitting on the floor, imagine your sit bones rooting into the ground. If you are sitting in a chair with feet on the ground, imagine your feet rooting into the ground.

With your eyes closed, picture heavy strong roots shooting from your feet, or sit bones into the ground. Allow the roots to go deep within the earth. When they are securely rooted, with every inhale imagine fluid, white light flowing up the roots and slowly through your body. On the exhale imagine the fluid white light slowly recycling back into the earth, and on the inhale, again, breathe in the light energy slowly through the body. Continue this cycle of imagery and breath for 10 minutes.

Books You Might Love

As You Think, Mark Allen & James Allen

You Can Heal Your Life, Louise Hay

A Course in Miracles, Foundation of Inner Peace

Miracles Now: 108 Life-Changing Tools for Less Stress, Gabrielle Bernstein

Your Word is Your Wand, Florene Scovel Shinn

Being Peace, Thich Nhat Hanh

The Miracle of Mindfulness, Thich Nhat Hanh

The Seven Spiritual Laws of Success, Deepak Chopra

Music for Chill Vibes
Sabrina's Chill Out Playlist

You can find and follow the link to my Spotify playlist on the resource section on my website.

www.sabrinajoatto.com/book

Some Social Media Accounts I Enjoy

Some of these accounts are famous figures and others are genuine people who have something special to share and light to spread.

Instagram:

Healthy is the New Skinny™ – Katie Willcox

Amanda Marit (Spiritual Coach)

Lewis Howes (School of Greatness Podcast)

Matthew Hussey – Dating Expert (but really the millennial Tony Robbins if you ask me)

Lexi Schaffer – Success Coach & Kundalini Yoga Teacher

Stephanie Williams – Raise the Vibe Yoga

Spirit Snacks

Dajon Smiles – The Mindful Veteran

Gabrielle Bernstein – Spiritual Teacher & Speaker

Sabrina Jo Atto - You can follow me too.
I would love to be friends!

❤ Acknowledgements ❤

Cheri Caddick, Writing Coach and Editor

Thank you for the encouragement to get this book started. Your feedback and support is ALWAYS uplifting and genuine. You have a way of making corrections and critique nonabrasive, and even empowering.

Karri Klawiter - Art by Karri, Book Cover Artist

It took one round of cover samples for me to love this one. You are so talented.

Miranda – Inner Circle Photography, Photographer

Such a fun spirit to work with! Thank you for your time and patience.

Carol Glover – Writer

Thank you for support and feedback on this project. Your help was beyond uplifting and meaningful.

T. Andrew Caddick – Layout Artist

Thank you for your hard work and support. This book could not have been completed without your talents.

Friends and Family

There are WAY too many people to mention by name but you all know who you are. I have the best family and friends, full of support, encouragement and anything else I might need when I need it! Love you guys! XOXO

♥ About the Author ♥

Sabina Jo Atto is a seeker. She is a teacher of yoga, a business owner, a writer and her passion in life is to help others heal.

Sabrina holds a Bachelor of Arts in Psychology from Oakland University in Rochester Hills, Michigan and completed her 200 hour yoga teacher training with Karma Yoga in Bloomfield Hills, Michigan.

Since completing her initial Yoga Teacher Training she has also completed training in yoga therapy, including Mindful Yoga Therapy with Susan Manafort, and Yoga as Therapy with Doug Keller. Sabrina went on to study Anusara Yoga in Maui with Skeetor Tichnor.

In 2013, Sabrina established Freebird LLC, a wellness coaching practice where she works with clients seeking a holistic or integrative approach toward healing anxiety and living a joyful life.

Web: www.SabinaJoAtto.com

eMail: YourFriend@SabrinaJoAtto.com

Made in the USA
Columbia, SC
30 September 2018